the urban hermitt:

"The Flow Chronicles"

Urban Hermitt: The Flow Chronicles

Published by:
Microcosm Publishing
Po Box 142332
Portland, Oregon 97293
www.microcosmpublishing.com
joe@microcosmpublishing.com
(503)286-1038

First Printing

ISBN: 0-9726967-0-9

Cover Artwork: Shawn Granton
Photo of Author: Subi Madly
Editor: Joel Cherney
Brain Drawing: Hermitt

Printed in Canada

special thanks to harmdawg. love, hermitt

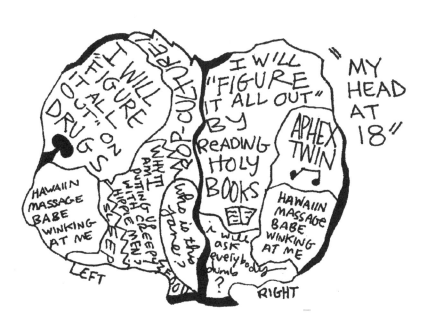

SOME PEON WROTE ME A LETTER:

Dear Urban Hermitt,

You have a lot to learn young lady. You can't just go around and make fun of other people's spiritual journeys, especially without the proper education and background. In fact, you have hurt me. I am a professional crystal healer myself and take pride in my work. For many years I have renewed peoples' souls and introduced them to many styles of healing. Yes, it is true that most of my clientele are women, but that does not mean that I sleep with them. Using the term creepy wanna-bee crystal healer dude in your writing only creates a negative association about crystal healers who happen to have deep respect for the YONI. Do you even know what the word YONI means, young lady? I'll clue you in. YONI means the woman's sacred spot. YONI is a much nicer word than the negative words you throw around like "cunt." If you claim to be a "Strong Woman" yourself then please stop disrespecting your sisters with degrading "cunt" language. Please stop making fun of the healers who worship them as well. It's a terrible shame that you are so negative, because you have so much potential. I can only hope that someday you'll find peace within yourself.

Love and Light,
Brother Kumbaya Love Chakra

4

1. THIS IS HOW IT IS:

Hi. My name is Hermitt. Not like a Hermitt who lives in a cave or is a wingnut saint. Hermitt, as in one of those weird names someone just has. On the 18th year and the 23rd day, *The New Age Gawds* (gawds=gods) came down to our fair Planet Earth, and said *you will be a weirdo for the rest of you life kid, therefore your spirit-artist name shall be the urban hermitt, or Hermitt for short.* I listened to what they said, thus beginning my strange life as a bitter kid who only really wanted to listen to The Smiths and drink coffee, yet was somehow attracted to crystal beads, everything Tim Leary ever said, tie die, and more. The New Age Gawds from the Sky also told me that after high school, it was my duty to go to a Liberal Arts College in the woods. Why does the college have to be in the woods if I am an urban hermitt? I asked the great New Age Gawds. They told me that it was part of the "plan."

What exactly is your plan, New Age Gawds? Humbly, I asked.

To be as weird as you possibly can be. They spoke. Ok?

I finally arrived at The Liberal Arts College in the Woods, a shy hippie boy by the name of Jeff, took me under his wing. He told me that the New Age Gawds came down from the sky and talked to him too. Well, he didn't literally say that (after all, I live in the imagination of my head, not yours, and not his) Instead, he smoked my brains out with pot from Southern Arizona, and took me on a walk. "This place is part of The Rainbow Family" he said, as we walked past the weird cement college buildings that were surrounded by thick green pine trees "Being here is part of The evolution of The Rainbow Family" he added on. I didn't know what he was talking about, but assumed that he meant that the New Age Gawds were talking to him too. "Jeff, what is the Rainbow Family?" I asked. Jeff explained to me that it was the coolest thing in the world, tons of the "brothers" and "sisters" gathered together and celebrated love. "When you are part of the Rainbow Family, you *know what's up* and that's the most important thing in the world Hermitt, to *know what's up.*" I nodded my head and pretended to know what was up like Jeff had claimed to, but still didn't know what in the hell he was talking about. Obviously, we were both possessed.

Jeff and I spent most of our time together eating pizza and watching The Simpsons on television. I am not sure if this is what the New

6

Age Gawds and The Rainbow Family wanted us to be doing? This behavior was the farthest thing from being holy. Didn't every kid in college eat pizza, smoke weed, and watch The Simpsons? Even my *riot grrrl Brooklyn-style-don't-fuck-with-me* roommate Loya, watched The Simpsons with us while eating pizza. Sometimes I would gaze away from the tv screen and look around Jeff's room. Tie dye was everywhere, so was marijuana art. His CD collection consisted of The Grateful Dead, The Black Crowes, Bob Marley, Nirvana, The Beastie Boys, Fish, and Led Zepplin. Usually after enough of smoking my brains out, I would go back to my place and stare at Loya's room. She had written the infamous punk band's The Dead Kennedy's Lyrics GIVE ME CONVENIENCE OR GIVE ME DEATH all over the wall. Her Cd collection consisted of every Ska band ever recorded and RIOT GRRL music which was quite a music battle from my The Smiths, Techno, and Gangsta Bootie Rap music collection. We battled everyday with our music. Nobody ever won. Loya and I were the tough asses of The Liberal Art's College in The Woods. Most everybody else lived in a land of tie die and The Grateful Dead. Most everybody was scared of Ska and Gangsta Bootie Rap music. All the hippies thought that I was going to kill myself because I wasn't always smiling, and I listened to Morrissey a lot. They thought Loya was going to kill herself as well. I tried to explain to all the hippie kids that the New Age Gawds came down from the sky and talked to me too! I was on a mission for Rainbow Love just as much as anybody else, I just happened to have good taste in music! (oooh! Ouch! Did I hurt anybody there?)

7

The real person who was depressed was my other roommate Joan, who moped around all day long wearing nothing but all black turtle necks and stretch pants. She never talked to anybody and I only ever saw her cooking microwavable pumpkin pies in the kitchen, then running back into her room to devour them. Joan ate one microwavable pie everyday. "Doesn't that seem strange?" I asked all the hippies. "Oh Noooo." They said, then passed me the bong. I tried to get to know Joan, simply out of human curiosity. The only things I ever found out about her were that she only listened to Prince, and only smoked menthol cigarettes. When I would go through reflective walks in the woods, The New Age Gawds would come down from the sky and tell me to be nice to Joan. So that's what I did: be nice to the person who is depressed and be neutral with the hippies (and fight with Loya!)

I never got to be friends with Joan in the end, though. I came home one day, only to find my roommates moping and crying. "What's wrong?" I asked. "Joan tried to kill herself! We were so surprised! We thought you were the one who was going to kill yourself Hermitt!" they spurted. Me, kill myself? Geez, just because I don't believe in smiling all the time and I like moody indie rock from England doesn't mean that I don't want to experience life for all it is worth. "You guys, I don't want to kill myself! I just like to be alone and read books." They nodded their heads and understood. It turned out that Joan, on the other hand, took 2 full bottles of sleeping pills and locked herself in the bathroom. When she was rescued, she got taken away and sent off to a Mental Hospital. It was kind of sad, but Joan's attempt at suicide brought my roommates and I closer. I told my roommates about the New Age Gawds telling me that I was going to be weird for the rest of my life. My roommates told me that they experienced similar things, but that the New Age Gawds told them more specially to believe in "one love" and live in the woods aka: we were all on way too many drugs. Whatever our trips were, be it: Dungeons and Dragons, Drugs that only *real* shaman should take, Dead Rasta Singers, or trying to write "The Great Amerikan Novel."

My trip was: One foggy night I took some majik mushrooms with all my friends and roommates. We drank it in tea form and then went walking through the woods once the chemical compounds seeped through our post-pubescent veins. We hugged trees and chanted hippie folklore gibberish. I looked up at the sky and saw pretty colors everywhere. It was nothing new, until we got out of the woods, and reached the parking lot for the dorms. My friend puked as I was simultaneousy was guided by a big blue shining **Hallucinogenic Egyptian Pharaoh that was in the parking lot calling out magic powers to me.** It spoke amazing things that I could never put into words. I could have been even more enlightened than the New Age Gawds. When my friend was done puking, the Blue Hallucinogenic Pharaoh went away. The next day, after I was no longer on drugs, I somehow decided that I needed to leave The Liberal Arts College in The Woods and move to The Big City, a few hours north. I didn't know why I felt this urge, surely I was possessed by Hallucinogenic Blue Pharaohs that made my friends puke; what did these drugs mean? That night, I got drunk and stormed around campus in a confused daze. Eventually, I ended up at Jeff's room. I sat him and down and said "Jeff, who am I? Am I an artist? A hippie? A poet? A kid? A freak? Who am I?"

"Well Hermitt," he softly spoke "you are just a person trying to *figure it all out.*"

A LETTER FROM A CONCERNED INDIVIDUAL:

Dear Urban Hermitt,

What is up with you making fun of hippie names? Don't you have anything better to do with your time? I was born with the name "Lavender Garbanzo Tea Tree." I did not choose that name, my crazy hippie parents gave me that name. My parents named my brother "Winter Lima Pine Tree" and did he have a choice with his name? NO! In fact, our families' last name is "Tree!" Yep, Mr. And Mrs. Tree are my fucking hippie parents! My whole life I have been teased in school for having this name. I can't change it right now because I am only 16 years old, still living with my parents, and since they are my legal guardians, they won't let me change my name. But I am not a fuckn' hippie Urban Hermitt! In fact, I don't know what I am! I do like listening to Tool, reading zines, and painting. But that doesn't mean you should make fun of people like me who didn't have the fuckn' choice to name themselves. Try living with parents who make you eat sprouted wheat-free bread, and won't let you eat cheeze! I hope you take this into consideration the next time you write something like a book.

Sincerely,
Lavender G!
(that's my homey style of saying my name.)
Marin County, California.

2. OLIVER TWIST AS A BOY DYKE:

The first time I moved to The Big City, I was taken in by the 27 year old hippie freaks. Strangely, the 27 year old hippie freaks were all single and did not bear any children like most other freaky hippies of the same age genre. You might say that is quite the contradiction to live in a big fat communal hippie house in the middle of The Big City, or as the freaky hippies would call "the concrete jungle," yet claim to be at *one* with the earth?

At the time, I was really into documenting the world around me into charts, so I made a HIPPIE AGE CHART, as to document the new 27 year old concrete jungle world around me. Here is what I came up with:

15 to 18 - the aspiring hippie will discover elements of hippie culture such as lsd, Tim Leary books, smoking pot. Activities include dropping outta school, or being stoned throughout school, playing hacky sac, etc...

18 to 24 - Full fledged hippie goes to Liberal Arts School in the Woods such as The Evergreen State College or The University of Santa Cruz or embarks upon full fledged hippie travels with an expensive backpack to places such as Europe and Southeast Asia to "find themselves."

24 to 35 - Have babies... OR grow out of hippie phase thus becoming a non-stereotypical creature or a hippie. Then there is a 2% rare breed of baby free urban hippies.

35 and on! - Congratulations! You've made it! You are cool as shit and hopefully right now, you are making black market bank selling your homemade herbs or prayer flags or maybe you are homesteading and growing your own organic cucumber crops. You are wise and have lived past the bullshit.

So, I was saying, I got rescued by the 27 year old urban hippies, who I really didn't know shit about. I just moved in with a few milk crates full of books and fell to sleep at night on a make shift bed supplied with couch cushions from the basement. Star, was the lady who actually took me in. She was feisty, bright eyed, and really spacey. But she was smart, the second I moved in, Star informed me that she was on a quest to become self employed by making didgeridoo outta plastic pipe tubing and that it was good that I had dropped outta college cuz there was too much shit to do on planet earth. *Don't let your parental units force you to be bored in school* she said. It was the first time anybody had ever used the term "parental units" in my wee life. "Parental Units" sounded so counterculture, so influential, and so Generation X even though I was more like Generation Y. And that's all I really got to know from Star, cuz in 30 seconds she was long gone in the basement scrapping away at the pipe tubbing and blowing funny noises into it.

I tried my hand at getting to know another roommate. Randy was the tall buttrock dude in a hippie disguise underneath a tie dye shirt and hemp necklace (just as I am really the disgruntled indie rocker hidden underneath a beanie and hemp necklace. We all know this game.) Randy was on a quest to become self employed as well, by making homemade candles and selling the green bud on weighing scales in his tiny room. One of the first things I ever learned about Randy was that by the time he was 17 years old, he had already taken 3000 hits of acid. I sure did believe it measuring by the high caliber of spaceyness that flew outta his bloodshot eyes. But then Randy put some of his "self employed" green bud into a colorful glass pipe and was winking at me with happy intent. I took deep hits and blew smoke out like it was not a drug that made me stupid, but an incense smelling thing that chilled me out.

Once stoned, I had to put on good music, you know? This called for one of the greatest techno albums ever made: "I Care Because You Do" by

Aphex Twin. So good. I was stoned, dancing, and trying to figure Randy out. By this time, he was at "the spiritual book library" in the living room. He was reading a book on the healing crystals of Sedona, Arizona. I browsed the "spiritual library" myself and came across the dirtiest, crustiest book I could find. I came across "Love Under Will" which was tattered in a blue cover with gold lettering and a gold symbol of some hoodoo voodoo design that I had no idea what meant. I flip to page one where the author claims that "she" did not write this book, but "god" transmuted special messages to her, meaning that "god" wrote the book. *I am merely a messenger and so are you* the book says. From this point on, I decide to only refer to this book as The Holy Book, since it's all about that shit to begin with.

<whoa, that's kinda cool that I'm a messenger too, oh holy book, but what am I a messenger of?>

In fact, we are all messengers The Holy Book says. I look over to Randy, staring away at the pictures of Northern Arizonian Healing Crystals, wondering what this cat was a messenger of... getting people stoned? Since he took 3000 hits of acid before the age of 17, did he know of secret universes, powers, and forces that I couldn't even imagine of? The Holy Book couldn't seem to answer that though, instead, it suggested that having a "god" talk to you was closer to "love" and "light" than taking 3000 hits of acid. Well, I'll tell you this, listening to Aphex Twin's "I Care Because

You Do" is closer to "god" than acid and crystals combined. And it was at that point in time, that the New Age Gawds from the Sky got replaced by The Holy Book. The Holy Book Reading Regime was Step Two in trying to figure it all out. (please use your imagination here, what I was going through could be compared to: switching from Sufism to Buddhism.)

It's just Aphex Twin, "god," and me... but then Star comes rushing up from the basement, and her world of plastic didgeridoo making.

"Oh Mi Gawd, is that Aphex Twin playing?" she shouts.

"Hell yeah" I proudly profess.

"Oh Mi Gawd, Jane used to listen to Aphex Twin everyday!"

"Who's Jane?" confused, I asked.

"Oh, Jane's my sister. She used to live in your room. Man, you really remind me of her."

"Just because I listen to Aphex Twin?"

"No" Star dazes "there's just something about you. Hey, you're really into techno, eh?"

"Yes" I said in this tone that expressed that techno music was indeed the music that kept blood doing it's pumping through my hella nervous heart. Yet, lots of people are into techno and lots of people are named Jane (thou saints and hairy men who live in caves are usually named Hermitt.)

"Whoa... hey Hermitt!" Star sez

"Yeeeeeees" my eyes roll.

"Are you a Taurus?"

"Why yes I am"

"Jane is a Taurus too, isn't that so trippy?"

I was about to say *Napoleon and my ex-best friend from 6th grade and yo' momma's 4th cousin twice removed are all Taurus too!* But I wasn't about to ruin Star's spiritual moment. Hey, maybe the Holy Book was already doing me some good. So instead, I say the classic words of "right on."

Right On is the perfect thing to say when you don't want to ruin somebody's spiritual moment. It's kind of like a halfway compromise between fake and real. I learned to say that when I went to The Liberal Arts College in The Woods. It' something you would say, if somebody in your class got up to read a nature poem that had good intent but was the worst piece of writing you have ever come across, and so you say "right on." Well actually, I didn't learn to say "right on" from The Liberal Arts College in The Woods, I learned it from the New Age Gawds.

See, the New Age Gawds told me to read books by Abbie Hoffman, The Black Panthers, and Tim Leary. All of them said *Right On*, and since they seemed cool, I used their language. But it was their language, so obviously I was missing the point.

SOME HUMAN SENT ME ANOTHER LETTER:

Yo Urban Hermitt,

You do not know me but I am a friend of one of your ex-bandmates out here in the ever so un-urban Eugene, Oregon. I picked up one of your old zines the other day and I really liked it. You have some potential there kid except that your spelling is kind of weird. On the other hand, I gotta check your shit. You say that your hippie days are of the past and that gives you the power to make fun of the hippies? What about the 18 year old hippies who are just like how you were when you were 18?!! Well buddy, your ex-bandmate tells me a few things about you. First off, she tells me that not only have you been seen making out with a girl in a tie dye scarf outside a co-op in Portland, and you have a habit of meditating on a regular basis, while burning incense from Nepal! She says, as well, that on Sunday afternoons you like to smoke pot and listen to Bob Marley! Maybe you have even participated in these activities today! Shame on you for making fun of the people who partake in the same activities as you! You ripping off people who need to read books written by real punks! You claim to be all "punk" urban hermitt so that you can sell your zines to a punk audience because zines are punk, not hippie. But

you are lying to these punk kids who "believe"
that you are some punk icon. Some kid is
probably thinking "that urban hermitt is so
punk rock" as they read your zine while you
smoke doobies with your tie dye scarf wearing
girlfriend and listen to commercialized reggae.
Whatever man.

-Anonymous
Eugene, Oregon
(Which is not entirely populated by
just hippies and black clad anarchists)

3. NO, THIS IS HOW IT REALLY IS:

Hi, my name is Hermitt. Not like a person who never leaves their apartment and has a hard time talking to people. Hermitt, as in a weird name, for a weird person. See, a thing known as "teenage rebellion" seeped into my soul one day and demanded that I be one big fat weirdo. "Teenage Rebellion" informed me that there were far too many boring people on the planet, and instructed me to do far too many drugs, die my hair purple, and try everything that has the word "radical" associated to it. "Teenage Rebellion" most often finds itself at All Girls Catholic Nun Schools, and that's where I found myself when I woke up from the daze known as: trying too hard to not be weird when you really are weird. I lectured nuns on radical theory, did book reports on Morrissey biographies, died my hair every color in the rainbow, and did everything that everybody was telling me not to do. It was 60 steps beyond James Dean and his "rebel without a cause" antics.

See, I won't lie to you about where I come from. I didn't grow up poor and I went to a private nun school. Maybe that may make you want to put this book down cuz I seem like a kid soaking in their own privilege. But hey! I just woke up outta my mother's womb one day, was fed a bunch of lies, and well, here I am! Ok? Everyday, I journaled and journaled as to why my current reality was full of nuns, goody twoshoe straight A student girls, and Republican parents. It was the stuff Joy Division and The Cure songs were made of. It has produced countless pieces of art just as much as people who come from tin shacks, ghettos, the streets, etc. Well, at least this is how I tried to rationalize my teenage rebellion.

Obviously, my family did not understand as to why Teenage Rebellion came to my soul and mindwarped me, for my sister went and told my mother that I was doing acid. I had never tried acid, so I dunno where my sister was coming from except that she feared Teenage Rebellion. Sadly, my sister's lies gave my mother the grand idea to go snoop in my room, read all my journals, and find a pot pipe! The pop pipe was quickly put into a plastic ziplock bag as drug evidence. And my mother went out and bought the book "Go Ask Alice" which documents what happens to this dumb girl when she takes way too much acid aka: she lets stupid boys fuck her, takes ludes, and in the end goes crazy and sees worms everywhere. "Go Ask Alice" is the stuff drama movies and afterschool tv specials are made of. My mom ate it and up and told my dad. At the time, I didn't know any of this.

At dinner one night, my dad took out a yellow paper pad and said "We have a health concern in the family, and do you know what happens when we have a health concern in the family?" I shook my head and said "No." Then my father jumped up and screamed "Well we have a health concern in the family and we are not supposed to have a health concern in the family! You are our health concern and we have to take care of it!" He ran upstairs to my room screaming like a wild caveman " I don't like health concerns arrrgh!" In my room, he went into my desk, took out a pot pipe, and said "See! See! Do you see what our health concern is?!!" He threw the pipe at me and then pushed me against the wall to the point that I fell to the ground, crying. He continued to ransack more of my room, breaking everything in sight. The next day I was put into re-hab for mildly smoking pot, and this is where I learned about drugs. You can get all kinds of drugs in rehab, and sending a pothead to rehab usually makes them realize that they don't have a problem at all! And that, dear reader, is where I come from.

A LETTER FROM A MORRISSEY FAN CLUB:

Dear Urban Hermitt,

Hi! My name is Myra and I am writing from The Morrissey Saved Our Life Fan Club. I just wanted to thank you for writing so much about how you love Morrissey, and The Smiths, even though your writing is more about trying to figure life out, making fun of hippies, and being a lesbian. Morrissey has saved countless teenagers in his time, and you writing about how he saved you will only further this movement. When kids are depressed and not feeling like they are understood, Morrissey and The Smiths songs soothe them. There are a lot of Morrissey-Haters on the planet who say that Morrissey is "a self centered man who only sings about being depressed." Well, the haters are wrong! Morrissey sings about being a human that needs to be loved, like we all do. Morrissey understands that we sometimes feel alone and there is no reason to hide it. Plus, he has really cute sideburns!

There is this really cool book called "Morrissey and Marr: The Severed Alliance. "By Johnny Rogan. You should check it out if you haven't had. The book is about Morrissey's life. Johnny Rogan goes and stalks Morrissey! There is one part where Morrissey wears black trenchcoats and decides to only hang out with lesbians. He had a black lesbian girlfriend too! He even wore pro-lesbian buttons on his trenchcoat! Morrissey used to also write for fanzines as he lived off The Dole and listened to Glam Rock. Way Cool! Well anyways, thanks for being a fan.

Louder than Bombs,
Myra O'Toole
Chief Morrsisey Worshipper
C/O The Morrissey Saved Our Life Fan Club
Albany, New York

4. THE CLASH ARE "SPIRITUAL":

A few weeks had passed living at the urban hippie house, and I was already into the groove of things. Calling into work sick at my Food Services of America Job, scoring a sac of psychedelic mushrooms from Randy, and calling up my friend Docia to invite her to trip the day away with me was exactly what the *groove of things* was. I soon discovered that my roommates didn't really pay rent making musical instruments, they paid rent by selling drugs. I wasn't a prime league drug dealer or anything like that, just a dorky young kid trying to "figure it all out." Is "figuring it all out" either understanding how manipulative people can be, or how spiritual people can be? For the past two weeks I had been wondering about this Jane kid and if her spirit was possessing my room, making me listen to more techno music than I ever listened to in my entire life.

Docia arrives at the urban hippie house in her thick steel-toe doc martins, her long Nine Inch Nails tee shirt, and tight black levis. Docia was hella bitter and hella goth. I hug onto her as she says "hi" as if she will help me "figure it all out." We take the mushrooms, mash them and mix them together with food bank peanut butter. In the living room, Docia and I dip carrots into the psychedelic peanut butter mix and wait for our brains to explode. Randy, being his usual un-employed self is on the same vibe and invites his friend Josh over to trip on some acid. This was already becoming an everyday reality too quickly. People really do live like this. Anyways, James was a high breed of woo woo. He never, ever talked in a non-soft voice. He was a professional house cleaner who always cancelled his appointments and the only way he ever asked the "ladies" out was to invite them for a massage exchange. Josh was all culturally appropriated dream catchers, Enya, and Sedona. Randy and Josh sat in the living room talking about the different kinds of healing crystals while listening to the buttrock band known as Rush, while Docia and I waited for the drugs to hit.

When I felt a slight buzz in my head, I grabbed Docia and said "Docia... I think it's time... I think it's time to head to my room!" I immediately put Aphex Twin on and began to read The Holy Book. But <surprise, surprise> neither the Holy Book nor the Genius Techno Music was helping me to figure it all out. "This is fucking boring" Docia mumbled in her hella-goth-I-am-a-student-of-Trent-Reznor-lyrics way. She was right, the so-called spiritual guidance tools were fucking stupid. Docia grabbed my hand and took me outside, to the backyard.

27

"Let's just... um, let's see... let's just, um... stare at the caterpillars in the dirt" she said, "stop trying to figure it all out hermitt"

It could have been hours, or a few minutes that Docia and I were on our knees digging in the dirt, staring at the caterpillars. I couldn't exactly figure out what the caterpillars were doing, but since they were being non-intrusive, it looked like they were doing something important. Ah yes, stupid young people on drugs. Was this what the counterculture wanted us to be doing? Were the makers behind "Dazed and Confused" and "Cheech and Chong" laughing in their business-executive chairs? Who was right, when you've already figured out that everybody's been lying to you for your whole life?

I bet the business executives in their chairs were saying: Ha! Ha! Those soul searching fools. They think they are all being "radical" when in actuality, they are doing what we are telling them to do. Ha! Ha! Har! Har! Paul, let's open up another headshop and sell more of those 30 dollar tie dye tee shirts with talking mushrooms on them! Ha! Ha! Then, we'll be able to buy the entire country of Lithuania!"

I had decided that the businessmen and the makers of "Dazed and Confused" would not get to me. Fuck this romanticism of Counterculture. "This caterpillar thing is boring Docia, let's go back to my room," I demanded. En route to my urban-hermitt-age bedroom, Randy and Josh slowly walked by and said "haaaaaaaaay seeeeeeeeester" ugggh. Bad vibes + bad vibes + bad vibes = wanna bee crystal healer dudes.

"Right on." I said, with somewhat of a fake smile.

To ensure optimum spiritual enjoyment, I was about to put the Aphex Twin CD back on, but Docia stopped me. "No!" she dictated "Fuck this hippie shit! We're putting on The Clash!" Wow, The Clash actually sounded really good once Docia hit <PLAY> on the CD player. I never thought I'd be rocking out to The Clash on psychedelic mushrooms, but reality has it's way of tripping things out. The Clash seemed to make more sense than anything. The Clash could kick any hippie's ass anyday! They made drug tripping alright, until my stupid ass looked in the mirror.

"Whoa, is that me, Docia?" The mirror was possessed.

"Yup." Docia was possessed.

"No Way." I was possessed about being possessed.

"Yup." Docia wasn't possessed about being possessed.

I couldn't take it, my face looked beautiful and alive in that mirror. So beautiful that it scared me, making the moment completely un-narcissistic. Like Nelson Mandela said "People are scared of the light that they project." So scared by own beauty, the mirror cracked! Right in front of my face! I ran outside to the living room in a state of Panic. Randy walked by, asking me what was going on. "The mirror cracked when I looked at it." I said, short outta breath. "Huh Huh" Randy snuckled "You know when you crack a mirror, that's seven years of bad luck." Now that is not the thing you want to say to somebody who is currently tripping on mushrooms. At this point, all I could do was sit on the couch in a state of panic. Docia followed me but was no help when all she could do was laugh. Laughing People On Drugs = Hella Annoying To Those Who Are Trying To Figure It All Out On Drugs. It produces the same feeling an uber thinking person gets when they walk back and forth through a super mall full of non-uber-thinking-persons.

No Holy Book could save me now. No Holy Theory. No "one love." Not even the random hippie folk walking into the living room, shouting "haaaay! Is Star here?"

"Uh... no... uh, I think," I barely said.

Docia kept laughing, staring at her finger. But she could have been staring at caterpillars or a jar of peanut butter, and it would have produced the same effect.

"Oh Hay, my name's Krist, well if Star isn't here I might as well stay and smoke." The random hippie said.

"Uh" I said. "Uh" means "Yes" in tripper language.

30

Krist was a tall bombshell, in society's sense. Skinny, tall, long hair, but urban boho hippie. Krist was also turning out to be the biggest pothead, loading green bud after green bud into a 3 foot bong. She kept offering some to me, but I horrendously declined, knowing that any more drugs would not do any good. Docia, on the other hand, smoked away like puff the magic dragon turned into a human in a Nine Inch Nails tee shirt. What would the counterculture think?

"Hermitt, what's wrong?" Krist inquired.

"Oh... uh... um... it's just um, that I'm having a bad mushroom trip. I cracked my mirror by staring at it and I need to come down," I said anxiously.

"Oh honey, why is it so bad? You just have to feel all the love around you."

"What if bad energy is all around you?" I snapped back, secretly referring to all the wanna bee crystal healer dudes.

"But honey, love will always fight out the negative energy."

"Then how come I can't do that?"

"Oh honey... hay!" the subject was now being changed since I didn't possess the love power. "Are you a Taurus?"

31

"Yes" how can all these people automatically guess my astrological sun sign?

"Yeah honey, I thought so. You know Jane, Star's sister?" Well, she's a Taurus too. Man, you remind me so much of her!"

"Why, becuz I am a Taurus and sleep in her old room?" I snapped back.

"Oh no babe, it's just psychic. You move and feel like her." Just after Krist said that, Star comes running into the living room, laughing the day away to the point that it is scaring me. Star asks me how I am doing and I tell her that I am on shrooms and freaked out by staring at myself in the mirror thus breaking the mirror thus cursing 7 years of bad luck. Star laughs hysterically, like is on the drugs too, and says "Yeah, that happens."

THE ESTABLISHMENT WROTE ME A LETTER:
aka: the facade of "the counterculture.")

Dear Urban Hermitt,

We are not fans of your writing nor do we care. Secret sources, however, tell us that you are writing a book on "trying to figure it all out." Whatever that nonsense means, we don't care about it either. We just want to let you know that we've already mind warped you a long time ago. Secret sources told us that you don't think you are "mind-warped" anymore. Such a fool you are my child! Secret sources tell us that you've been buying our glow in the dark "tobacco" pipes, watching our movies like "Dazed and Confused" and "Dude, where's my car?" and being a sucker for the "munchies." "Munchies" is a marketing term that we made up and if you don't stop writing these preposterous books on "trying to figure it out" we might just have to trademark the term "munchies." Besides, modern day media, we have brainwashed you even farther, oh yes we have urban hermitt. We did the same thing to Allen Ginsberg, mind warp him, by putting him in khaki commercials for The Gap. We programmed Tim Leary, a man people believed to be a hero

33

for consciousness, to be a womanizer! We even blackmailed hip hop diva Queen Latifah, to lie to the public and say that she is "heterosexual." OH GASP! And we can do it to you! Watch yourself.

Sincerely,
The Mainstream Hippie Businessmen of Los Angeles California

5. MY JOB AND ANCIENT CHINESE HEALING HERBS:

At the "juice bar," (my current Food Services of America Job position) I was basically assigned by the corporate-esque food service manager named Mitzi, to stuff pieces of fruit and globs of concentrated orange juice into a blender to make smoothies for all the office workers of the 100 story building. I was always fascinated by the thick, ugly brown bottle of liquid ginseng that lay next to the blender at the "juice bar." The bottle looked romantically ancient and was written only in Chinese. As Mitzi would yell at us to be "team players" I would daydream that this bottle was Edgar Allen Poe's magik juice, and that only wingnutty poets and tribal sufi mystics were to drink from this bottle. Yeah. It's the team players verses the wingnutty poets. This form of imaginative thinking helped me cope with that fact that I was instead feeding liquid ginseng to yuppies and getting paid weak amounts of dinero, to pay rent to the drug dealing hippies.

I was tripped out on the ginseng root like wicked mad. My spacey hippie freaky roommates, more specially Star and Randy, would munch on big chunks of ginseng root and start talking things like "the manifestation" and "the Mayan calendar splendor" They made this ginseng root seem holy especially since they always looked massively bug eyed, like a tranced-out shaman. (from this point on I thought that hippiesh folk who dumpster dived and mooched off the government would help lead the revolution, leading us thru the concrete jungle armed with Chinese healing herbs, ready to make tea, not war) Yet in my 18 years of existence, I had not yet sampled the root of ginseng. it was much easier writin' poetic crap and fantasizing about it.

But back in Mitzi's corporate food service land, I decided to pretend that the spirit of Edgar Allen Poe and some sufi mystic preferably named "xtallian lightin' bolt" would channel through my veins and force me to take many, many shots of the pure liquid ginseng. Much more exciting to dabble in these unknowns than the typical "run into the alley and smoke as much weed as you can" tactics that I had used to bear the froth of food service-ism. Needless to say, after a few minutes of downing the ginseng shots with the ample pace of a sorority girl taking vodka shots, a whole new realm of time space, and reality hit me. I felt as if I was living in a box and my brain and soul was merely a floatation device for a higher powers. "Mitzi, I

36

am having a paranoia attack" I mumbled as if everybody would merely think I was stoned again. "What's wrong" Mitzi fumed "it's the lunch rush, goddammit" "Mitzi, I need to sit down."

I sat down on a milk crate in the back room and tried to figure out why I felt like my soul was a box, and how I couldn't seem to come up with wingnutty poetry or sufi mystik visions during this experience. Usually these people seem to have these experiences on mescaline/ lsd/shrooms/etc... not ginseng! Shit damn! Was I schizo? Or the reincarnation of some force I couldn't understand? All my co workers asked what the problem was. I told them that I had drank too much concentrated ginseng extract. They all laughed. "It's only ginseng," Mitzi fumed with her subtle nazi powers. "Get back to work now!"

When people say "I am re-born" I believe them! that's cuz i get reborn all the time, yo! Not this "it takes me 7 years to get new cells" crap. Not a bible. Not a cult. Not an identity crisis, but realizing that there is more for you to realize!! Spirlulina makes me feel like there are so many new ways to communicate with plantlife! Juicing oranges, apples, and ginger root and toastin' the juice with my roommate Star helps me realize that health is way cooler than these stupid fantasies of whiskey drunk writers or tripped out ravers. I get re-born on licorice tea. (realization that tea rules!) I get re-born when I go dumpster diving (realization that you don't have to pay for stuff) I get re-born when I gather with friends and we come up with movements like "call, write, or e-mail everybody you know and tell them to call, write and e-mail everybody they know with the message: on November 3rd, 2005... let's all smile and hug each other at precisely 5pm pacific standard time! go!"

I even get re-born on ginseng. it's easy to get re-born you know, when it's sunset and you have an awe inspiring song stuck in your head and all you do is smile at the sun melting into the sky, thinking thoughts like "whoa, dude... it's peace!" and as much as I bitch about Corporate Counterculture and the large population of humans who be all IDIOT, I really do think many thoughts like "whoa, dude... it's peace"

EXHIBIT: a tripped out college drop out who is walking down the street, smiling, and saying "hello" to all that she passes by. The people that she passes by, not only ignore all possibility of smiling, they don't even look each other in the eye! This saddens the young, tripped out food service brat, when all she wants to do is think thoughts like "whoa, dude... it's peace!"

"Yo Mitzi," I ask one morning at the juice bar, "why is it that people seem to ignore each other when they walk down the street?" Mitzi pinched my cheeks like the corporate nazi that she was and said, condescendingly "oh, look at you, you're sooooo cute, you're just like me when I was your age, don't worry you'll get over it." Mitzi was 27 years old as well, just like everybody in my life.

38

"Oh honey, you could be such a cute thing, but look at you" Mitzi said, now stuffing a Burger King breakfast sandwich into her mouth. "honey our boss likes to call you the little rag muffin so maybe you could get some better fitting pants." Arrgh! This is my pet peeve numero uno! Anybody who tells me that I have to get tight clothing thus taking away from the holy thang called COMFORT. "Mitzi, I need to have extra wide leg room comfort in order for me to properly distribute the smoothies" I sarcastically responded to the corporate food service diatribe. Mitzi stormed off to the hot dog place every time I said this. I didn't get a "20 cent raise" because the food service drones thought my pants were too "big."

Oooh, how I despised the enigma known as Mitzi. She was everything I despised about corporate lesbian-ism. She was the reason why I was scared to come out. Mitzi tucked in her corporate shirt with her pant going up almost to her neck. Mitzi also had a mullet! why! why! why! how many more freakin' lesbians must have mullets? Don't they realize that a favorite pastime of punk dykes is to go mullet watchin? I was scared that if I got enough courage to admit to the 27 year old hippies that I was really a dyke, I'd automatically grow a mullet. The mullet would attack me in my sleep!

Each morning when I would chop up the pineapples and concentrated orange juice globs at the "juice bar" (and fear the wicked ginseng bottle) Mitzi would troddle her 400lb body whilst stuffin three hot dogs in her mouth. Now I don't care if Mitzi was 400lbs or not, for I am not a skinny kid myself and chunk is way beautiful, it's just that Mitzi's 400lbs were made up of hot dog fat. That's all. "You want some" Mitzi said every damn morning with food still in her mouth." I don't eat meat, I'd tell her for the gizillionith time. (My life story is about pretending to be vegan and vegetarian even though I am really just that sad kid in an animal rights tee shirt stuffing a piece of salmon into their face.) However, "meat" as a concept, was not considered a tool to help you "figure it all out" for the urban hermitt.

Revenge, however, was to take place. After the brutal <your pants are too big for my corporate image of fast food restaurants that call burritos "wraps"> arguments, Mitzi would assign me to the cash register at lunch instead of the juice bar as a torture tactic. "Here's two bucks" I would say when giving change. I tried to give the customers a casual experience at the cash register to keep things low stress. Mitzi didn't like this. Every time I said the word "bucks" instead of "dollars" she would march on up and make a big scene in front of the entire office worker population of The Big City... tellin' me that the word "bucks" sounded like I was an "un-educated hick" No, Mitzi... actually, that's "a do it yo freakin' self sneak into college libraries in theory anarchist to you Mitzi" An Urban Hermitt does not equal an uneducated hick.

40

Needless to say, I soon learned a valuable life lesson: you can quit your job anytime you want! Shortly thereafter, I learned another valuable lesson: I could quit my job, but due to the powers of poverty, and that I couldn't seem to make any money selling drugs, I was forced to get another Food Services of America Wage Slave Job the following week.

COOL PEOPLE WRITE ME LETTERS:

Dear Urban Hermitt,

This is a letter from The Pro-College Drop Out Union. My name is Vick, and on behalf of the P.C.D.U., I'd like to congratulate you on not staying in college. There are many, in fact most people that you probably will meet, who will tell you that you are bad for dropping out of college. They will tell you that you are destined for a life of shitty food service jobs. They will tell you that you will never make it in this world without a degree. While, they may have the freedom to say this, this does not mean that all who drop out of college are destined to be using the cash register at McDonald's. Have you ever considered a career as a Hemp Businessman, Self Run Book Distro, RockStar, Sufi Dancing Instructor, or even writing a book? Yes, it can happen! We here at The Pro-College Drop Out Union have a vast amount of brochures explaining what you can do in the world without a college degree. We have guidebooks on how to run your own business, how to build musical instruments, and much more. We just want to let you know that you will not be stuck at shitty food service jobs for the rest of your life. Please spread the word, and never forget that there is a world beyond pieces of paper and "prestige."

In The Name of Self Education,
Vick Ozwana/P.C.D.O.U.

6. AND THIS IS WHEN A THANG KNOWN AS "CREEPY HIPPIE MEN" STEPPED INTO MY LIFE.

There is a certain topic that has long since been ignored, in thanks to the over population of Amerika's butt-rockers and *liberal arts school going indie rock Murder City Devils culture banging mid 20-ers obsessed with white trash culture:* they forgot the dred mullet! Now I know you might be thinking fuck hermitt! I'm so sick of people talking about mullets, this is pop culture burnout! And believe me, I am a bit overly toasted on the GPC smokin' Camaro diggin' Megadeathin' Mullet Heads myself. But have we forgotten diversity? Here in the world of pop culture, the midget mullets, lesbo mullets, un-pc mexi mullets etc have all been represented while denying the spotlight for our dreadmulleted friends.

Exhibit: Dolphin. The roommate at the communal hippie house who was never home. In fact, I hadn't even met him, until tonite. He was a professional traveling hemp salesman. He was a combination between a rasta Michael Bolton, a burn out, and a yuppie. Aka: the rasta Micheal Bolton syndrome that just won't give up. Dolphin was a nymphomaniac, I had soon discovered, as he stared at my chest. You could see the pain in his eyes, and this is why Dolphin hung on to his dying, festering dreadlocks. It's this neo-hippie-philosophy of: *chicks will dig me if I have dreadlocks and portray the image of a wanna bee crystal healer even if I am balding, have a mullet, and don't know shit about crystal healing.*

Hmmm. How do dreadlocks or the "illusion" of being a pseudo crystal healer lead to great sex? I was soon to find the answer to this question. After 5 minutes of meeting this new housemate, Dolphin had informed me that he had acquired some opium and invited me to go upstairs to his room and smoke it. His room was highly populated with dangling crystal beads and hemp products ranging from *hemp ginkgo hawthorne berry granola,* to *hemp stress reliever lavender soap.* Truth be, opium sounded so artistically romantic to me at the time. I blame this all on going to a Liberal Arts College in the Woods. Even though, every time I smoked opium, I ended up staring at the wall, drooling on myself, and horridly listening to The Grateful Dead. (The Grateful Dead only seemed to make sense to me when I was doped up on opium). Nonetheless, I lit up the black tar opium with Dolphin, thinking that maybe this would be the point when my life would

be artistically romantic, like a French
philosophy book... and...

My life was like a french philosophy book.
Dolphin was morphing into an asshole-istic
wanna bee French philosopher who kept telling
me "when I was your age, I was just like you"
"oh yeah, I've been there and done that." I was
about to say to him no you haven't and my life
destiny isn't to sell hemp granola except that
the opium had fucked me up to the point of
drooling and craving the hymns of jerry garcia.
This sucked, cuz I lost all intellectual defense.
I was just a dumb drooling kid who happened to
have breasts which delighted Dolphin.

"You have some big breasts" he seethed.

"So what?" I grrr'd.

"Can I touch them?" he slimed.

"Hell No" I double grrr'd.

"But big breasts like yours need to be
touched." He creepy-fied.

"Fuck off!" I yelled and ran away into my
room. Dolphin wasn't the first creep to hit on
me at the communal hippie house. In fact, this
shit happened all the time, and it was getting
old. I had heard things from hey baby, what's
your sign to your room smells nice, it smells
like you. How was I ever going to become a fully

functioning boy dyke if I had to keep fighting off the forces of creepy men who just couldn't get a clue? Well, I slept on it. When I woke up and wandered into the living room, Dolphin was "massaging" Star's breasts on the couch. It was so gross, that I went back into my room and slept some more. This word "massage" is used way too much for the wrong reasons.

During my second attempt to wake up, I wandered into the living room again. Dolphin was gone, thank you Buddha! But, Star was still there. "Star" I asked "why did you let Dolphin play with your breasts, he's hella creepy you know."

"I know he's creepy" she said.

"then why?" my soul bled.

"Because he's lonely and needs to love like anybody else." Well that was true, but I was lonely too, and I needed love like anybody else. So how come sexy girls like Star weren't playing with me? Why are all the babes all over nasty asshole men while the tomboys get left out in the dust? It was like Dolphin was the gross rich rap daddy pimp on an MTV rap video and Star was the babe in a bikini humping him with gold and caviar, except that this was hippie style. What was that icky feeling that I was smelling in the air?

"You know, my sister Jane didn't like Dolphin either. so it's okay. I just choose to see the good in him." She said, like she was the Holy Book.

46

"Oh..." not this Jane Thing, again! Jane! Jane! Jane! Taurus! Taurus! Taurus!

"You know," Star said "Jane's bisexual. She came out in this house. It was really hard for her. But I knew who she was all along, so when she came out, I was all like girl, I knew all along, no worries."

"Oh." Was it obvious to Star that I was really a stone cold butch dyke in an earth mamma hippie disguise? And if this was obvious, then why were the male creeps hitting on me? Male creeps need to admit that they are gay for being attracted to me, that's what I tell them before they tell me that their dick will make me a real woman. What is a real woman? Curse these breasts!

"Hermitt, I'm glad you're still a virgin, it's good."

"How'd you know?"

"Cuz you don't sleep with any of the men who come through here."

"Oh." Did Virgin mean Lesbo in Hippie World?

People shock you all the time.

A NEANDRTHAL WROTE ME A LETTER:

Dear Urban Hermit(t),

First off, I don't know if you've ever heard of a Microsoft Spell Check, but "hermit" is spelt with one "t," not two. Of course that is not a major problem. But, calling yourself an "urban hermit" does not quite make sense. Doesn't a real "hermit" live alone in solitude? And doesn't a real "hermit" usually live in such places like mountains, caves, and the countryside? I don't see how a "hermit" can live in a big crowded city, sleep in communal houses, and always be in contact with many people. A real "urban hermit" would live alone, never leave their home, and not write huge, horrendously misspelled stories about all the people that they meet. Maybe you are trying to convey some "deep" message that nobody understands to ensure yourself a "deep artist image." But I don't buy it. You may have fooled the masses but you sure have not fooled me! Why? Because I am a real hermit! I live out in the countryside on a farm. The only time I ever see people is when I am at the gas station or at the supermarket. I suggest in the future, you try living a true "hermit" lifestyle before making a claim to fame.

John Meyers
Oskoshbagosh, Wisconsin

7. CREEPY MEN DON'T HAVE TO BE HIPPIES, THEY CAN RIDE SKATEBOARDS TOO:

There is a power that I have that maybe a lot of you will never have. It is the power of being an adult tomboy: I can pass as a man 50% of the time, and as a woman 50% of the time. There is power in holding my shredded skateboard on a rainy night, walking home, and knowing that nobody will fuck with me. They see the baggy clothes, the baggy hat, and the board, and they think that I am trouble. No one fucks with trouble except the Po Po. Little do they know that I have plans to go home tonite, drink tea, and try to read some Holy Books. I ain't no thug,   I just like the thug music and the thug fashion. No more drugs, ginseng, and creepy men named Dolphin for me! I had that power and then some dumb kid holding a skateboard as well, has to run up to me and scream "hay bro." When I say hay back he realizes that I am a girl, and I lose my power, cuz now he is saying he remembers

49

me from some party (which means that he is hitting on me) and says "Hey my name is Ivan, and since I remember you from that party, do you want to hang out." I shrug my shoulders, cuz I just lost that tomboy power, and I want it back but then Ivan says "I just got paid and I'll buy you some alcohol." I just got paid and I will buy you alcohol were two very important phrases that I couldn't refuse. I took Ivan to the supermarket, handed him over a big ol' bottle of red wine, and smiled.

Ivan was small, wore nerd glasses, and looked like a rat. People are always very funny when they look like rats. It was a J.R.R. Tolkien novel come to life. The whole way walking back to my hippie house, Ivan kept talking about how he worked all day and just got paid and wants to party with this money. I ask him what exactly he does to get all this "money." "Oh, I work for an internet service." He says. "Yeah, but what exactly do you do there?" "I pack boxes" Ivan reluctantly said. I told him not to feel bad because I used to make juice for businesspeople, but now I wash pizza pans. When I arrived at my house, and walked into the living room, there was a posse of hairy shirtless hippie men pounding drums and smoking weed. "Haaaay Seeeeeester" they all said like the creeps that they were ooga booga to the max. I grabbed my bottle of wine and went to hide in my room, like a good urban hermitt. Ivan followed me in, and I tried to entertain him by playing all my hip hop records. Ivan claimed that he was really into the hip hop, so I was trying to bond. Well, Ivan didn't really seem to give a shit about my records, and leaned in to kiss me instead. I pushed him away and let out a big ol "NO!" like they do in Self Defense/Karate school where they kick down plastic dummies. Ivan just wouldn't let me have any of my tomboy powers. Skateboys, why are you scared of the tomboy power? Skateboys, why do you make girl skateboard shit pink? Cuz you are scared? Ivan didn't talk about my baggy hat, my hip hop records, my skateboard. I wanted to go play in the woods in some treefort, and Ivan wanted my pussy. He must have been really desperate cuz when I denied him the kiss that he thought he deserved, he left my room, and went out to the living room to hang out with the creepy men which was a blessing, cuz I then turned out the lights, and went to sleep.

It must have been 4 in the morning when Ivan came into my room and asked if he could sleep in my bed. "Hell no" I said. He convincing argument was that the buses weren't running so he couldn't get home, and that the living room was full of people sleeping everywhere. I informed him that he couldn't touch me, couldn't cuddle, but he could sleep in my bed. Then I turned over and went back to the comfort of my pillow. The pillow was a good friend in those hippie times. A few minutes Ivan was tapping at my shoulders.

"What?"

"I just jacked off, where should I put my cum?"

"Don't fucking stick it on my bed."

Ivan then dripped his cum into his dirty striped red sock, and looked over at me with very large pupils. I asked him why he couldn't fall asleep. "Oh, I just tried speed for the first time tonite."

"Why in the hell did you do speed?" vigilantly, I asked, without realizing that I had currently been doing every drug in the book as well.

"Your roommate Randy makes and sells it, and since I got paid, I thought that I might as well try it, you know?"

Oh Gawd, not only was a very annoying rat boy waking me up during my precious sleep hours, but he was telling me that my roommate was making and selling speed: the most fucked up drug in the universe? That was enough to make me want to go back asleep and forget about all the stupidly in my waking life. Maybe the dreaming life would offer full trays full of tropical fruit, sexy babes licking my fingers, and cool women-made hip hop blasting through solar power speakers. That'd be cool, wouldn't it Ivan? Ivan? Ivan, Hello? why are you staring at me and rubbing your cock? Why are you disrespecting my tomboy powers? Ivan? Do you want me to ride a pink skateboard? Why can't you talk to me in the spiritual realm? There are no gender roles in the spiritual realm.

"Hermitt, I know you're asleep but I wanted to

do you a favor." Ivan said.

"Yo Ivan, if you let me go to sleep, then you'll be doing me an awesome favor."
"Oh come on, just one favor, all the ladies love it when I do it."

"What is it?"

"Just let me touch your cunt a little bit, I swear all the ladies love it when I do it."

"Ok, you can do it a little, but I am not doing or giving anything to you." I said. I decided to milk Ivan for all he was worth. I wasn't attracted to him at all, but I sure as hell wanted to feel good. So, Ivan stuck his creepy little fingers and touched all around my clit. It didn't feel good at all, I just kept giving him this pessimistic bored look. He kept trying and trying, but honestly it felt like a misguided robot was trying to mutilate my clit. Stop the rats from invading my holy cunt!

"You don't love what I am doing?" he asked as if I was supposed to fucking worship his rat ass for rubbing his messy fingers everywhere? I laughed. I didn't say any words and just kept on laughing. Ivan stopped touching my clit, got up, put his clothes on, and left looking very sad. Oh well, that's what you get when you don't listen to my hip hop records, acknowledge that I skateboard, and understand that I am just like you except that I have a pussy. Dig?

A RAP SONG I WROTE JUST FOR YOU:

I first met you at the Recycling Center.
Your tee-shirt said you were a "Green Party Member."
You were eating apricot flavored cliff bars.
You came here by a vegetable oil run car.
Then I met you at some protest rally.
Coulda been in Santa Cuz or Berkeley Cali
I let you taste some of my vanilla soy milk
Since you worked at the local co-op, you said "girl, that's ill."
I let you drink it outta my reusable mug
it had stickers about free mumia non-monogamous love
after the protest, let's buy some bell hooks tickets
and talk about free love empowerment kisses
But I'll have to part soon, so don't be balling
Once fall hits, I'm gonna go to The Evergreen St. College
But for now I could some hippie hemp lube
And some crystals that mean shit dude
I even got a book on the tantra
it's deep man, like the earth mamma
let's listen to some techno sitar
and plant a save the tree farm
we all be culturally retards
cuz we got a pc kind of love
i even let you fuck on my culturally appropriated rug

8. BEFORE THERE WAS THE RAT, THERE WAS THE TROLL:

Hi there again. I have a confession to make: I am a Scam Artist Wanna-Bee! In Hiding, I admire those who are able to return clothes without a receipt, live off credit cards, and more! Oh, but I had my ways. You the confession is that I already knew about the existence of creepy hippie men before I moved into the Urban Communal Hippie House. Back in the summer before The Liberal Arts College in The Woods stole my soul, a "job" known as Telemarketing was currently busy stealing my soul. It was actually more like "Telefunding" than "Telemarketing." The job title didn't matter, however, because i hated every minute of it. One day the boredom of telefunding was killing me so bad that i had to sneak off to the park to smoke some pot before going into work. In the bushes I hid, and was about to take out my DANK PRODUCTIONS-esque pipe. A chubby hippie man then came outta the woodwork and whipped out a huge ziplock bag full of weed. He offered to smoke some of his weed on a log, so i quickly hid my pipe, and joined him. His name was Troll.

Troll began to ask me who I was and what I was about. I told him about hippies, Janis Joplin, and my bad love poetry. "But no Hermitt, where do you really come from?" He asked. I admitted that my dad was a big stinking lawyer and that I was glad to be leaving his house and onward to the Liberal Arts College in The Woods. "That's right" Troll said "Your father is the maaaan! The establishment! I know his law firm and I'm gonna rip them off!" I didn't believe him. In fact, i believed the trees more than i believe him meaning that I got up from the log and stared at the trees. When I stopped looking at the glorious trees, I turned my attention back towards Troll only to find him jacking off! His turkey looking dick was flying everywhere. "You sure are cute!" He kept saying.

"Fuck off!" I yelled. Troll's response was taking his cum from his wrinkled looking turkey penis and dripping it into his empty Pabst Blue Ribbon Beer can, and then drinking the beer can! I said about a million more *fuck yous* and ran off.

A few months later when I was doing time at The Liberal Arts College in The Woods, my roommates and I were driving towards town to go to The Vet to cure our little kitty who was illegally living in the dorms. Alongside the highway, a chubby hippie man was hitchhiking. He was holding up those *Role Hemp* stickers that were a parody of *Dole/Kemp* running for president in 1996. We picked him up. When he sat down next to me I realized that he was Troll who drank his cum in front of me in the park. "Do I know you?" I seethingly asked. "No" he said in this really dumb *oooga booga* tone.

"Are you sure I don't know you?" I kept asking. Troll kept denying it. My roommates told me to shut up. When we dropped Troll off, I told them the whole story. The car got silent. Little did we all know that the rest of that week, Troll would be parading around The Liberal Arts College in The Woods Campus trying to sell those cheezy *Role Hemp* stickers. Every time I saw him I yelled FUCK YOU like the lil' riot grrrl that could. All the hippies got scared when I yelled. Soon everybody on campus thought I was depressed.

Upon my escape from The Liberal Arts College in the Woods, I began to take big long walks around The Big City. I walked to all the bookstores that had "spiritual books," headshops, incense shops, and coffeehouses. Today, I had just purchased bulk patchouli oil at the downtown markets, like a good baby hippie. Walking through the hustle and bustle, I noticed that there was a man in the distance selling more of those *Role Hemp* stickers. The election had already ended. Bill Clinton was our president, so why was this person selling these outdated stickers? As I drew in closer, I noticed that the fellow turned out the be Troll! I screamed my classic FUCK YOUS! He laughed in my face and said "What are you going to do about it kid?" And then, my street smart powers kicked in while all the *hippie bullshit* temporarily left my system. With these powers, I punched Troll down to the ground with my *shaking-*

57

because-I-drank-too-much-coffee-today-fists, and then ran as fast as I could through all of downtown. Rain poured. Buses were late. Creepy men were all over this city. I went home to my room to hide.

AN OFFICIAL LETTER:

Dear Urban Hermitt,

This is a letter from the National Council for Rigid Gender Binary Systems, writing to inform you that your recent application for "A Non-Gender-Binary-System-Universe" was denied. We did a background check on your physical body, and due to the fact that you have a vaginal opening, and breasts, we could not let you exist outside of our Rigid Gender Boundaries. Sorry, but that is just the way things around here work. Tomboys stop existing after the age 11. When young ladies turn 11, we expect them to start dating boys and shaving their legs! You have been struggling against this for 12 years now! Shame! We can imagine that you may be upset, but you must understand that this decision is for your best interest. In the future, you will soon discover that people who fit in our Government Sponsored Rigid Gender Roles, will have an easier time existing. Those who are heterosexually married will get cheaper car insurance, tax breaks, and more. Those who fit our McDonald's sponsored Rigid Gender roles will not get harassed all the time, will have bathrooms specifically designed for them, (ie: women/man restrooms) and will have clothes, toys, and movies specifically catered to them as well. You may not believe us, but current rap star Queen Latifah was received a warning letter from us as well. She did what we suggested (for her own benefit that is) which resulted in us giving Queen Latifah her own talk show for wearing pink. Are you familiar with celebrity Martha Stewart, the lady who makes her own crafts on TV, and writes *Martha Stewart: Living Magazine*? Well, we are the reason she hasn't come out as a "lesbian" yet. We told her to follow our Rigid Gender Roles, and now she has her own TV show and magazine. Would you like your own TV show and magazine Urban Hermitt? If you take our advice (that is for your best interest, of course) you too could be making lemon pies, x-mass gifts, and interviewing people like Tom Cruise on Television! So remember, we go way back in time, Urban Hermitt. Remember that Joan of Arc person that all the "gender benders" worship? Well, we are the *real* reason why she was burned at the stake.

Joan of Arc is Dead,
Kendall Walters
Associate Coordinating Director
The National Council for Rigid Binary Systems
Dallas, Texas

9. IN ACTUALITY, I SPENT MORE OF MY TIME DREAMING OF PUSSY, THAN ACTUALLY TRYING TO GAIN ENLIGHTENMENT.

Do you know what I mean when I say "pseudo-girlfriend?" I don't mean "just friend" and I don't mean "long-term-smooshy-butt-partner," I mean that kind of friend who seems more than a friend when they start cuddling in bed with you, holding your hand on the bus, and kissing you in the dark hours of the night, in secret. Have you had one of those? I'm sure you have. Maybe not "pseudo-girlfriend" but "pseudo-boyfriend" or "pseudo-fuck-buddy." Yes, dear reader, I am sure you have had one of these, nasty-yet-oh-so addicting things.

My pseudo girlfriend was named Natasha and she did not like that I had moved into an urban hippie communal house, emphasis on hippie, at all. Natasha was more obsessed with gay boys in

61

gap clothes holding starbucks coffee cups and sucking frat boy cock, than my patchouli stinking drum circle reality. Needless to say, she wasn't cuddling with me every night. It felt like the relationship had broken up, which was kind of good, cuz I was sure as all hell, sick of having a fake girlfriend. I wanted to taste pussy, not the breath of an in denial lesbian who's been too busy sucking frat boy cock. Or maybe Natasha was bisexual. Bisexual and totally denying it.

Then Natasha came back into my life. Freshly dumped by another frat boy "boyfriend," she came knocking at my door like a puppy without a water and food bowl. Nastasha hugged me, groped my ass, and somehow convinced me to go shopping with her. Shopping was not what you did in the urban communal hippie house. It was against the current-hippie-belief system and "figuring it all out." Hell, I only bought drugs and holy books, dig? But due to the fact that Nastasha was cute and was groping my ass, I came along.

Today's shopping journey was to take place on Broadway, the big main gay freak ten thousand piercing and goth stores where everybody and their mom hangs out street in the heart of The Big City. Nastaha was in her "fag-hag" stage. We went to store after store, flirting with her preppy gay boy friends, and browsing the clothes. I sat in the dressing rooms watching Nastasha try on sexy clothes while I bit my nails and tried to deny my sexuality. Living in fear that if I came out as a lesbian, then I'd have a mullet. I listened to Nastasha rant "I'm too fat" as my beer belly stuck out way farther than her beer belly. Yes, she was great fake-girlfriend material. The stuff bitches are made of. It was only when we got to Urban Outfitters at The Gay Mall, that things didn't stay BORING. Stacy, Natasha's friend from the local community college, was busy shopping too, holding up a big disco ball party light thingee. "Hay gurl" Nastasha said fresh outta her bitchy lips "what's the disco ball for." Nastasha swung her purse. Stacy flipped in her hair. This was so like an 1980's John Hughes movies. "Well Nastasha" Stacy said "It's for this big huge killer party that my friends are putting on you so have to be there! It's gonna be rager. Dj's and shit." "Cool, Hermitt and I will be there" Nastaha said, in a bossy way, assuming that I was going to go to this killer party with her.

But fake girlfriends will have their way. I was dragged to the party, which was better than shopping and schmoozing it up with gay boys who used to be frat boys at the local Starbucks near you in The Big City. Who was I to complain? The party was alright when we got there. A DJ spinning some De La Soul. An empty dance floor but a bunch of cool kids smoking pot, and Stacy and other assorted raver kids coming out of a bedroom, sniffing their noses. There were raver kids in pink visors. Raver kids in ninja outfits. Raver kids in dreadlocks. I even met a raver kid who was a cheerleader at the local high school in The Big City. I interviewed the Raver Cheerleader extensively, as to break free from my bad stereotype of that all cheerleaders are stupid. But then the raver cheerleader stops answering my questions and shouts "it's him!" All heads at the party turn over and direct their attention towards a tall lanky man in a black trenchcoat and gold chains. Kinda like a goth-pimp, eh? "Who is he?" I ask, since everybody is worshipping him like he's either Tupac, or Gawd.

"Oh" The Raver Cheerleader peeps. "He's here to deliver the E." (E = Ecstasy in raver drug language)

"Oh"

Nastasha comes up to me and pinches my ass, again. "So Hermitt, you wanna try E?" "Oh, why the fuck not" I reply back Maybe taking ecstasy would help me figure it all out, maybe ecstasy would even help me understand all those Holy Books I've been reading or why I'd trip out on things like ginseng. Just Maybe. In hopes, I hand over a hard earned 25 bucks to the man in the trenchcoat and he hands me over a little tiny pill that looks like any ol' aspirin. I pop it in with a little tap water and wait for the drugs to hit. All the Raver kids are smiling. They keep telling me that I am going to love Ecstasy and once I taste it, I'll never go back. I started to think about that girl Jane for a bit, you know the girl who used to live in my room at the hippie house? I wondered if last

64

year at this time, Jane was taking E at house parties and dreaming of good techno music. But then again, I also wondered how many kids across the world were doing the exact thing as me. It didn't make the whole occasion feel any special.

I sat down on the living room floor and still waited. A bunch of kids were waiting on the floor as well, as if some Holy Leader was going to come. And then... the drugs hit me. I was alive and everything tasted good. I turned over to another kid, smiled, and kept on smiling. Within those few precious seconds, I began to understand RAVE CULTURE. That made everything worth it. Standing behind me, though, there was a very skinny girl with bugged out eyes who was shaking. I asked her what was wrong, to which she replied "what are you guys on?"

"Why...Ecstasy!" A bunch of us replied, like the rave party had just begun.

"Oi Mi Gawd, all you guys are on Ecstasy???!!!"

"Yup" We all smiled.

"Oh No, all you guys are on ecstasy! Noooo!" She freaked "I'm calling the cops!"

After that, the worried, shaking girl made a mad dash to the phone to call the police while faggy little raver boys on way to many drugs tried to chase her. But it was too late, she had made it to the phone. Upon this not-too-cool information, the girl who was hosting the party gets up on a table and screams "GET THE FUCK OUTTA MY PARTY NOW, THE COPS ARE COMING!" Nastasha grabs me and we jet to leave. The girl hosting the party stops and us and sez "Oh, you guys can stay here, you're Stacy's friends." "NO!" Nastasha growls, like the bitch she is. We go the bedroom where the coats are only to find Stacy and her friends sniffing as much Blow as they can outta a Dollar Bill. Stacy looks up at Nastasha and I, as we get our coats, and says "I'm sorry." She wasn't sorry about the cops, it was about the coke. Stacy was a cokehead just like my roommate Randy was a methhead. The People Are on Drugs, and Nastasha and I are outta the party in a quick second.

But wait, Nastasha and I are on The Drugs. And it doesn't really occur to me how high I am until we reach outside, where there are lots of big fuzzy trees to space out at. "I like the trees" I told Nastaha, to which she replied "Hermitt, look at the lights!"

"Huh?"

"Look at the lights over there"

I looked up in the sky and saw a huge radio tower blinking red lights. It didn't seem as impressive as the few, rare trees left in The Big City, but Nastasha didn't care, she was tripping hard. All that came outta her lips was "The Lights... The Lights." Which was no help cuz I wanted to get home or at least not get lost. I knew the navigational skills were up to me. We walked for awhile, until a tiny man came up behind us. "Haaay Ladies" he said "My name's Patsee." Nastasha said "Haaay Patsee" back as if she could not tell that this Patsee fellow was a conniving creep who only wanted pussy.

"Hay Ladies, I work over at the fried chicken place at Westlake Center downtown, you should stop by and get some free chicken." He slimed.

"Oh Yeah totally, hey check out the lights" Nastasha said back.

It was at that point that I realized Patsee had followed me home last week when I was walking home from work. He tried to offer me free fried chicken as well. This was no good. I kept trying to wink to Nastasha, to inform her that this guy was a creep and that we should be getting away from him. You know, that silent look with a little bit of nervous eye roll, when you want to communicate bad news to somebody without using words. I kept winking and winking and Nastasha kept saying and saying "What is it Hermitt, I don't get it... what?"

"Hay Ladies, you should come back to my place" Pastsee added.

"Sure dude, right on" Nastasha the dumb ass said.

Ahhhh. Pastsee kept following us all over town. When we finally reached the local ghetto mini mart, a large man with no teeth starts running at us screaming "I'm gonna get you, muthafuckah, I'm gonna get you's Pastsee, gimmee my rock back!"

I grabbed Nastasha and ran. Pastsee decided to run behind us. Then, the toothless man screaming "I'm gonna get you Pastsee" starts running after Patsee. They are running faster and faster, to the point that Nastasha and I can't get away. I gatta think fast. Street smarts somehow overpower the drugs I am on, and make me a sly-tv-show-style motherfucker. I swear. I look up to my left and see that there is a party going on the second floor of a house. So, I take a left and go up to the party, to hide. Is that what a real life action movie is like?

Nastasha and I mingle in with all the party-goers drinking their champagne and eating their stinky gourmet cheese. But then I remember that I am on ecstasy and head to the kitchen to get water. You have to drink a lotta water on E. I find the biggest glass jar possible and fill it to the brim with fresh H2O from the tap. I decided the call the jar the "majik jar" since it will contain the very fluid that will help me not die or get a heart attack on drugs. "Oh Majik Jar" I say "You are..." but then I get interrupted by Pastsee who has just arrived at the party. It seems he has just discovered that this is where Natasha and I have been hiding. I panic but then Pastee takes out a big ziplock bag full of coke and starts dealing at the party. Ha! I take this as my cue to leave the party and get Pastsee outta my life. "Natasha, we're leaving" I demand. "No" she says . "Come on, we gotta get away from Pastee." "No." I told Natasha to fuck off andthat I was leaving without her. I dash out of the party, and start walking down the stairs and guess who I see? The big toothless man who was out to get Patsee. Big and Burly, he comes running up the stairs screaming some cracked out gibberish. The street smart powers start to kick in me, like crazy mad, and I end up punching the big toothless crazy man, and he falls down the stairs. I swear this is all true. I look down at my fisted hands and thank them kindly for these wise street smart powers that have overcome the power of mind altering drugs. Thankful, I decided to run in and rescue Nastasha by force. She doesn't want to leave, but I drag her anyway, trying to explain the whole Pastsee-toothless man-drug dealing-situation. We hit the streets and walk for hours. I am neither Superman nor Superwoman, I am simply a 30 second SuperBoyDyke!

During our street walking, I kept checking myself out in window reflections. Not in a vain way, but in a self reflective way. Everytime I look over, I see a nice kid. "Nastasha, I am a nice kid, a good person" I say. Nastasha laughs and says "Well, I'm a cat" She didn't get it, but finally, I was having one-of those-awesome-self-realization drug trips. I was becoming The Holy

Book and it was a good thing. I can't put it into words, but it was a good thing that I was on this drug. It was getting rid of my ego and telling me that I was an alright kid. Too bad I had to take drugs to realize this.

When we got back to my house, I was uber excited to put Aphex Twins "I Care Because You Do" as to not only cherish my favorite techno artist, but to listen to some good music after a hard night. After I pressed play, though, Aphex Twin sounded dark and scary. My favorite techno music artist was giving me a bad trip! It was horrid. I kept trying to listen, but I couldn't. it was then that Nastasha said "Hermitt, you should just put on The Cure" Another hella-goth friend to the rescue.

"Goth music on an Ecstasy Trip?" I asked, all shocked, even though just yesterday, so it seemed, I was tripping on mushrooms with a bitter goth head who made me listen to The Clash.

"Trust me" she winked.

I put on The Cure's "All Mixed Up" and it sounded so good. Crazy. I felt so good, I put on my crazy purple hippie hat, grabbed some pastels and paper, and started running around the house and drawing! It was my playground goddammit, until my roommate Julie came home. She was the bitter as all hell roommate who was moving out of the house at the end of the month because she couldn't stand all the roommates. Meaning, Julie was never home. I didn't even know her just like I really didn't know Dolphin. "You know what the problem is Hermitt?" Julie said as she stormed in the living room "the problem is that this house is going down hill. You'll see."

"ok!" I said in a really high voice that gave it away that I was on drugs.

"what's up?"

"I tried ecstasy for the first time tonite. It's crazy"

"yeah" Julie said, as she lit up a menthol amerikan spirit cigarette "Jane used to do a lotta ecstasy."

Oh No, someone else was going to talk about Jane too. I could see it all coming. Maybe Jane would magically appear outta a cloud of fresh smoke as Julie compared me to this kid, then it would all begin to make sense. Julie busted out the classic lines that I had been hearing everyday now... like "Do you like Techno, oh Jane likes techno." "Are you a Taurus? Oh, I thought so, Jane's a Taurus"

"Julie" I said, firmly "everybody's been comparing me to Jane. It's getting ridiculous, I don't even know who this kid is? And just because I listen to techno music and my astrological sign is a Taurus, doesn't mean I am her twin!"

"Of course not." Julie said, through a thick cloud of culturally appropriated cigarette smoke. "You just remind me of her, that's all. She's gay you know."

"Oh" I said, all shocked, as if Julie was all too aware of my fake-girlfriend-ship with Natasha. The air got silent. Julie changed the subject.

"Do you like my iguana?" she asked, pointing to Barney, her mellow iguana who sat peacefully in the living room.

"Yeah, he's cool. I wonder how much pot smoke he's consumed."

Julie laughed. "Well I keep him healthy by feeding him spirulina everyday. You know, Iguana are amazing creatures. They are of a higher consciousness, more higher than any human can achieve. I'm going to bed now."

Julie put out her cigarette and left the room. I spent the rest of the night turning into morning, staring at the Iguana wondering what it was thinking, as Nastasha lay soundly asleep in my "Taurus rave music gay room." The Iguana was at peace but then again, the Iguana does not have to deal with crackhead lunatics either.

A LETTER FROM THE ELECTRONIC MUSIC GENERATION:

Dear Urban Hermitt,

Why do you glorify Techno music and the drugs that are associated with it so much? Did you know that Techno music is responsible for some of the worst music on the planet today? Consider Haddaway's "What is Love? Baby don't hurt me, don't hurt me, no more" song, as featured in the Saturday Night Live Film "A Night at The Roxbury." That song is awful! And it is played everywhere! I can't even go to a club anymore and have a decent dance without that song being blasted.

Techno music is also responsible for "the remix." This is where crappy DJ's have to take a good song, and mix it with really bad backup gospel singers, and fast drum machines! "The remix" has also produced a large amount of wanna-bee Whitney Houstons and Paula Abduls. This is not a good sign of where humanity is going, now is it?

Another thing Techno music is responsible for is The Bad Pop Music of the year known as 1989. Consider Mini Vanilli, who didn't even write their own songs. Consider also, Ace of Base, who gave the country Sweden a bad reputation for decent music after their "All that she wants is another baby" song. RuPaul, Technotronic, Snap, BlackBox, and more came out that year as well.

And if it could even get worse, it does! There is even a bad techno song about Barbie! It seems apparent to me that the makers behind this sad genre of music are on drugs. And not good drugs.

Consider, if you will Urban Hermitt, the music known as Death Metal. This is a fine caliber of not only strong-nordic-craftmanship-guitar-playing, but mighty lyrics about our castle-Nothern-European-poetic roots! Appreciate, Death Metal if you will, Urban Hermitt. The only drugs Death Metal Musicians are on is Beer! Beer is not responsible for bad house music, crystal methamphetamine is! Death Metal Music also expresses people's true emotions. We are not a happy human race, so why not listen to the songs that truly represent us.

Enclosed is my Band "Luficer's Dead Baby's" demo Cd. Perhaps you could book us a show in your area?

Death Metal Pride,
Keith "Lucifer" Bates
Clearwater, Florida

10. A BACKGROUND CHECK ON MY RELATIONSHIP WITH NATASHA:

One year ago was a long time ago. Lemmee tell you a story about who Natasha used to be, cuz see: We were free as we thought we were supposed to be, driving 90 MPH in a beatdown white car (looking like something that James Dean would ride alone at night when he was frustrated) cruising through an island just north of the Big City. Natasha and I had almost runaway from our parents but due to social pressures, we graduated high school first and then we ran away. This was before Natasha became a preppy Abercomie-and-Fitchin' fag hag, and before I was taken in by the 27 year old hippies. Stoned and in a ripped up Phish shirt, I thought I had it all figured out. I believed in hippies, white kids with dreadlocks, 4:20, and anything in between. With this cocky hippie-centric attitude problem, I was going to show

Natasha the naked hippie hot springs retreat center on the north side of the Island.

Cruising right along the countryside highway, I noticed there was a tall bald man in a tie dye tee-shirt hitchhiking on the side of the road. Natasha and I pull over to pick him up. Once he gets in the car, I notice that this bald fellow in the tie dye tee shirt is seriously wearing 15 hemp necklaces on his neck, and is sporting death metal tattoo all over his tanned body. He told us his name was Wally and that he wasn't really going anywhere, he was just out for a journey. Wally then took out a book that looked like a Holy Book: weird symbols and a language that most Westerners could never understand written on the front. "This book has guided me," Wally said "I have given up my possessions and wandered. I guess you could say that I am pretty much enlightened." Yes, it's really true, Wally actually said I am *pretty much enlightened*. I smirked while Natasha, without asking me, invited Wally to come along with us on our journey.

"How old are you guys anyways?" he asked.

"18" we said "and how old are you?"

"27."

27 seemed so old at that time, that if I were less of a bitter person, I woulda believed that Wally was actually an enlightened person. Well, upon Natasha's knowledge that Wally was over

the legal drinking age of 21, she convinced him to purchase alcohol for us. The old car did a turnaround, post-poned it's journeys towards the naked hippie hot springs, and headed towards the small town in the center of the Island. Wally did the deed for our 18 year old nourishment, and walked outta the liquor store with a gallon of the cheapest rum known to humans in a plastic bottle. Whoo-weee. Even though all the people who were probably seriously enlightened like the Buddha didn't consume alcohol whatsoever, we silly hippies thought that we could still be enlightened and drink cheap rum outta plastic? How ridiculous. The language we were using. Words like "peace" and "the way" and "the one" while we were gallivanting around this tiny innocent town like drunken fools. Natasha then, whispered in my ear "Wally thinks you're cute, I just know it." I didn't know if that was true, but if so, it made me feel good. Even though I secretly didn't like biological male loving and secretly lusted after Natasha every moment I could get, the possibility of somebody thinking that I was sexy sure felt good. I winked and nudge nudged at Wally the whole drive back to the naked hippie hot springs retreat center. We set up a tent and re-opened the plastic jug of the econo-core rum. The sun was going down and life felt good. Or maybe the sun couldn't haven't existed, and the liquid drug was the thing that was making me feel good. Wally felt really good too, cuz then he felt the urge to come up to my ass and slap it. "You have a nice ass" he said. He went up to Natasha's ass after mine, slapped her chunky derriere, and said "You have a nice ass as well. In fact both of you have really sexy asses." We all took another shot. Then Wally must have felt super-dooper good, cuz he felt the urge to take out his hard cock. And now, not only did Wally claim to be *pretty much enlightened*, but he claimed to be really *well hung* as he swung his cock all around in the air. We all took another shot. Then Natasha must have felt more super dooper good than simply being super dooper good, cuz she said "let's go into the tent, to... uh huh... sleep." We all snuggled in and began to cuddle away our drunkenness. Shit, are we really going to have a ménage à trois? Oh mi gawd, is this really happening. Sex with a girl and a boy and I'm still a virgin. Whoa dude. I reached down and started to rub my cooch to the pleasures of being young, stupid, and alive. But then... I heard voices. It was Natasha. "So, that's what kind of kisser you are" she sure as hell wasn't talking to me. She was kissing Wally! I tried to move in, but nobody wanted to kiss me. Before you knew it, Wally was sticking his supposed "well hung" cock into Natashas shaved pussy. I ran out of the tent in a sad, pathetic, drunken rage. But I am human and I need to be loved like Dolphin too, I say!

I roamed around the entire hippie hot springs retreat center like a demon in the night. Everywhere I looked, everybody was coupled. *Heterosexual! Heterosexual! Heterosexual! Heterosexual!* Man and woman making out in the hot tubs. Man and woman making out on the beach. Man and woman making out in front of their tents. Even though I was jealous of all the couples, even some Woman-Woman/Man-Man action would have soothed the situation. Finally after running around everywhere like a madman, and being short of breath, I climbed up to a treehouse that was adjacent to the tent that Natasha and Wally were busy fucking in. At the top of my lungs, I began to sing The Door's greatest hits. The question is, did I sing the entire album? Who knew? I was angry. The hippies wooed my outta tune singing on. But I don't think Wally nor Natasha like The Doors, cuz Wally comes jolting outta the tent, shouting "Hermitt, what the fuck are you doing? Get back in the tent and get to sleep." He demanded. "Noooooo! Not until you guys stop fucking in front of me!" I screamed. Wally then climbed up to the treehouse and transported me back to the tent, as if I were an infant. I probably was.

It is not a shock to say that the next morning was not a friendly time for the urban hermitt. While Wally and Natasha were busy smooching and poking each other like it was too cute to be alive for them, I was busy puking and cursing the empty plastic bottle of rum. "Damn, you crazy" Natasha said, in my face. Well, life was crazy and I didn't know what the hell was going on. Wally announced that he had a "500 dollar paycheck" that he could pick up today and that he wanted to keep traveling with us on our journey, more specifically, he wanted to go to a big hippie arts festival that was going on in the big city. "I'll pay for everything" he said. This produced big smiles and immediately put Wally at pimp status. Him fucking my friend that I wanted to fuck didn't seem like such a problem anymore. Still hung over, I jumped in the back of the old beat up car, and Natasha drove to Wally's home in the woods.

Wally and 3 other guys had set up their own illegal tent city in the middle of the woods, right next to a big creek. 10 minutes away was a vacation resort that they all worked at. Wally announced that he was quitting his job today so that he could come on a journey with his. I wish I could have trade places with him and lived in his rent free tent city. Instead, I got dragged along to the resort, where Wally found his boss, pointed to Natasha, winked, picked up his check, and said goodbye. Near the ferry dock that would take us back to the mainland of Bigger cities and The Big City, Wally cashed his check at the local mini mart. With wads of cash inside his culturally appropriated Guatmemalan pants, Wally took us out to eat at the most expensive restaurant there was on The Island. He ordered a big steak and a thick rich dark beer. Natasha and I looked stunned, assuming that anybody who claimed that they were pretty much enlightened would be a vegetarian, raw foodist, or somebody who didn't eat things like steak. But Wally said "Boy, I sure love steak. People usually think that due to my spiritual beliefs, that I don't eat steak. But I am a spiritual guy, I just sure love my meat."

On the ferry ride, Wally announced that not only was he *pretty much enlightened* and was *well hung,* but Wally also told us that he was a *musical composer of life.* With that, he took out his guitar, paused, and told us that he had been working on an amazing song. He said that this song was the song that explained everything. Natasha and I listened with great intent when Wally began to play. He strummed and strummed playing some basic short melody, and then he sang: *are you there? Do you care? To see me smiling!* He repeated those lyrics over and over again to the point that he almost cried. Aaah, it was the cheeziest song I have ever heard in my life. I said "right on" when Wally was done playing, but rolled my eyes at Natasha the whole time. *Ugh, if I say Right On one more time, I'm gonna hafta turn into a motivational book therapist for recovering hippies!*

The meat-propaganda-love-fest continued when we got off the ferry on the other side, and Wally told us to drive to a hamburger joint at the top of the hill. We weren't in the Big City yet, just another Small Town. We inquired why we had to drive all the way to the top of the hill to eat hamburgers. Wally told us that we should just trust him since he had the money. Yes, he was my hippie pimp and I didn't even have to suck his cock. At the hamburger joint, he slapped high five with all the employees, and chow downed two hamburgers.

"See that guy flipping hamburgers in the back" Wally said "we're going to his house in a few minutes." And it was true, in a matter of minutes, the kid who flipped hamburgers was riding in the back of our old beat up car. His name was Justin and, according to our hippie pimp, he was going to hook us up. Hooking us up meant stepping into the basement of an dingy house into a cloud of weed smoke while The Chemical Brothers blasted on the stereo. Stoned butt-rock dudes were everywhere to be found. Natasha was scared. She was the only girl (hey, I am not a girl in most situations, I am the tomboy which is never the girl. Or in other words, I am not the one the straight guys wanna fuck, I am another dude. A dude with a pussy) all the creepy stoned men tried to hit on Natasha while all they tried to do with me was smoke me out. During all this, Wally went into a backroom with Justin. Five minutes later, he came out with the largest ziplock bag of weed I have ever seen. Wally smoked everybody out and then we were off to The Big City.

The only place to stay in The Big City was at my parents' house. They lived more so in the suburbs but were closer to The Big City than being in The Islands or The Small Towns. I wish I could say that I didn't live with my parents, but hey I just graduated from high school and was only 18. Natasha was living with me for the summer, sharing my room. Which was really hot and really, really torturing. But this time, she didn't sleep in my room. She slept on a pull out couch with Wally in the tv room. They fucked the night away while my parents had no idea what was to come to them when they woke up. Natasha instructed me to lie to them and tell them that she was sleeping in my room, Wally slept alone, and Wally was an old family friend of hers. That was a pretty non-convincing argument when my ever so Republican parents stared in utter horror at all of Wally's death metal tattoo. "Oh, a friend of Natasha's family, yes I see" my parents said all suspiciously. We took it as our cue to leave the suburbs and head on out to the big hippie folk music fest.

Wally paid for our admission, smoked us out every 5 minutes, and even bought us an entire pizza. The pimp-ness was coming into full effect. When I said I was thirsty, Wally would buy me a Pepsi. When Natasha said she was tired, Wally would light up another bowl. In fact, Wally was everybody's pimp. It seemed like he knew every hippie at the festival and would smoke all of them out. I met Real Life Rastas, Dead Heads in wheelchairs, Women who believe they were Fairies, White Trash Hippies, and all that. Wally was also his own pimp. He bought himself cookies, clothes, and a brand new sheepskin drum. With this drum, however, he began to sing his "special" song that he had already sang on the ferry. Accompanied by basic hand-drum pounding, Wally sang out loud, *are you there? Do you care? To see me smiling.* Over and over again. He even sang it all the way back to my parents house when the festival ended, the sun sank, and it was time to go to bed.

The next morning, the house seemed empty. I walked outside and began to kick a soccer ball around. It was fun and a good time to be alone as my parents snored away and Wally and Natasha fucked. You could say that the moment was all "la, la, la." I didn't expect reality to turn into one-big-pain-in-the-ass when my neighbor came outside and starting screaming at me like a christian fundamentalist preacher. "Youz all a whorehouse! Youz breeding prostitutes!" he yelled.

"Excuse me sir" I spoke "but what are you talking about?"

"I saw your demon friends having sex with the window open! That's prostitution. I know you guys are breeding a whorehouse in there!!"

"What are you talking about?" I said, again. I figured he had seen Natasha and Wally fucking, but whatever this whorehouse jargon was about, I had no clue.

"I'm telling your parents about your whorehouse and I want you to leave!"

I ran inside and hid in my room. Urban Hermitts hide in their room, you know. Luckily, a few hours later both my parents left without seeing the fundamentalist neighbor nor Wally and Natasha. I tippy toed into the tv room to wake my nasty friends up. I told them about the crazy neighbor incident to which Wally replied

84

"let's get stoned." We smoked and Wally played his stupid are you there do you care to see me smiling song. He played it for so long, that the annoyance prompted Natasha to stand up and say "Enough! We can't mope around here all day, let's do something!" Wally still had some of his pimp hippie money left, so he suggested that we hop on a ferry across the water and visit his parents. It wasn't something I was dying to do, but since Wally was currently classified under hippie pimp status, I went along anyways.

Inside the beat up old car, Natasha couldn't even turn the key to make the car go. We were that stoned. I tried to drive but I couldn't do it either. Instead, we ended up laughing hysterically in some stoned gibberish. Wally decided to pay for a taxi to the ferry dock. This was pimp city baby. On the other side of the water, Wally got another taxi to take us all the way to his parents government subsidized apartment. Yeah, this was uber pimp city baby.

Wally's parents were really spacey, but not in that hippie way. When we came in, they were sitting on styrofoam coolers and watching the christian fundamentalist channel on the tv. All the walls in the apartment were blank and there were these styrofoam coolers everywhere. Wally's mom made us ham sandwiches (ok, so I ate meat when I was free), and then we all stared at each other with absolutely nothing to talk about. Wally's parents went back to the tv and Natasha and I ran into the bathroom to talk to each other. "I don't know about this Hermitt" she said "I mean Wally has a big dick and all, but he's starting to get really annoying and his parents are weird." "Let's just see what happens" was my response.

When Natasha and I got out of the bathroom, we heard some acoustic music. What was it? We walked forward a bit some more only to find Wally picking 3 simple chords on his guitar and singing *are you there? Do you care? To see me smiling.* "Uh, Hello Wally" I said. "Oh hey you guys, I'm practicing this song cuz I'm going to play it for my parents" he said, excitedly. Wally went up to his parents, turned to tv off, and said "let's talk."

"what should we talk about Wally we haven't seen you in 10 years" they moaned. 10 years, whoa!

"But I am here now!" He said it in this way like he was the prophet of the now.

"Then what have you been up to, Wally?"

"I am a *musical composer!*" Wally exclaimed. Oh gawd, I could see the stupidly coming. Geez, I write stories, but I would never call myself a composer of stories.

"Oh really" his dad said "can you play us something?"

"You sure bet."

"Then I'm gonna go get me my tape recorder and record you my son." His father said. And at that, Natasha and I were forced to listen to more than our life's share of stupid folk music. *Are you there, do you care? Are you there? Do you care? Are you there, do you care? To see me smiling.* His parents smiled. They were so spacey, I couldn't tell if they were fake smiling or real smiling. It was so sad, that after not seeing his parents in 10 years, all that Wally had to show for himself was one song that he wrote, and a bad song at that. Natasha whispered to me again "at least he has a big dick." So what if anybody has a big dick? I have a **big dildo that's bigger than your big dick,** and it does the same job! If I ever hear the phrase at least he has a big dick again, I am going to go to the fridge, take out a cucumber, and shout "see!"

We spent the night at Wally's parents house. The whole night I got to hear more and more of the powers of Wally's supposedly big dick. Ugggh ugggh ugggh moan moan moan. I hoped his poor parents didn't hear the loud hippie love fucking going on at the subsidized government apartment complex way out in hickville USA. But I'm sure they did. I felt so icky about the situation, that I didn't even masturbate, and I masturbate everywhere I go. We left in the morning, Wally's mom driving us back to the ferry terminal. Wally went out to the deck and played more of his song. At this point, all I could do was laugh and laugh. "Hey Natasha" I whispered "Do all enlightened people play the same song over and over again?" We smirked and smirked. But he's well hung! 8 inches! Natasha squealed. Where was my bag of vegetables and all women-run sex toy shop when I needed them?!

It was when we got off of the ferry when Wally broke down and confessed that he was all out of his money and that we would be taking the public bus back to my parent's house. At the bus stop, Wally took out the very last bud of his pot, smoked it, and pouted. "It's all gone" he said. Natasha fake smiled. I was starting to wonder if that just because Wally was 27 and I was 18, didn't mean he was more enlightened than me. "Did you know that I have a kid" Wally gloomed "I have two kids in fact, but I don't know where they are, their mom is a bitch."

"oh" Natasha and I said. I was beginning to think that **aha!** maybe a lot more 27 year olds than i thought had babies, and they just weren't telling people because they were too busy trying to tell people how enlightened they were!

When we arrived back at my parent's suburban home, my father was standing at the front door with his arms crossed. "Well Hello" he said, in very mean tones. Then he turned to me with a big red face, called me by my real name, and said "Can I talk to you privately." Uh oh. My father laid down the law. He wanted Wally out, he wanted Natasha out, and he wanted me to apologize to the fundamentalist neighbor. He wanted them out now. "But we have no car" I humbly said. "Your mother will drive them to the Greyhound bus." My father demanded. So goes being 18, young, and free... eh?

I told Wally and Natasha the news to which Wally replied "See I am such a loser! I fucked up again! I'm running away" like a big baby. Wally ran outta the house. We chased after him as he kept screaming "I am such a loser." Well, it didn't seem like Wally was pretty much *enlightened* at all. We chased him all the way down to the waterfront where he threatened to hijack a canoe and paddle back to The Islands. Eventually we got Wally and brought him back to my parents' suburban house. Then my mom took us to Starbucks at a strip mall where soccer moms and housewives seethed at the death metal taboos all over Wally. My mom bought us Frappucinos, and drove Wally to the Greyhound station. Wally cried and cried and informed Natasha that he would be writing musical compositions on the guitar to express his deep love for Natasha. "Oh that's the sweetest thing anybody has every said to me" she said. I smirked and knew that she really wanted to say *Oh Wally, , I am going to miss your big dick because I don't even know what all women run sex toy stores exist and I don't like cucumbers!*

A PERSON FOR SOCIAL CHANGE WROTE ME A LETTER:

Dear Urban Hermitt,

I have a bit of a concern with your book talking about your sexuality too much. Now, don't get me wrong, I am not homophobic. I just don't understand why you have to put your sexuality in your book. You are more than your sexuality, urban hermitt, you are a person. If it wrote a book, I wouldn't call it "masculine straight white male bad speller fictional shakespeare writer." I am a communist-anarchist, a vegan, and a fighter for social change before I am a masculine straight white male. The message for social change is much more important than who we fuck. Labels will only trap you and make you stagnant. Of course, if you choose to be gay, then you should have the freedom to love who you want. But you are a person, urban hermitt, before you are gay.

In Solidarity,
Wayne Schmidt
C/O The Northwest Communist-Anarchist Freedom
Fighter Collation for Social Change. Eugene, Or.

11. FINDING ENLIGHTENMENT OVER A MCDONALD'S CHEESEBURGER:

Natasha got a real boyfriend who wasn't a frat boy whatsoever. In fact, Natasha's real boyfriend was best friends with my roommate Randy, meaning he was a buttrock-hippie. This meant that Natasha was now an everyday reality in my life. This also meant that Natasha was on a high time mission to remove us of our pseudo-girlfriend status. She was trying to hook me up with her boyfriend Colin's other best friend: David. David was a biological male and didn't have a pussy. What was I doing? I hadn't really told anybody that I was a flaming homosexual yet, but I thought maybe they could just figure it out with mine and Natasha's fake-girlfriend-ship-hood. I was "supposed" to hook up with David, that's what everybody was telling me. David was a buttrock hippie too. He drove an alfalfa sprout truck for a living but only ate the sprouts on cheeseburgers. That's a good explanation for a buttrock hippie: sprouts on burgers. He was ok, but I didn't want to grab his balls and direct them into my bushy little thing, by no means.

Part of Natasha's mission to hook me up with the biological male, was to take a "camping trip" to the coast. She said that leaving The Big City would be good for us. Colin, Natasha, David and I all gathered up our shit and head off for the coast in David's big ol' red 1973 Dodge van. David drank franzia boxed wine the whole time, drunkenly driving thru swervy roads while Natasha and Colin annoying made out in the back, saying annoying things like "I love you smooshie pookie pumpkin butt." Fools in Love I thought. I was jealous. I wanted to taste Natasha's bush and I thought I deserved it. It wasn't my fault that I was a masculine creature born in a woman's body. It wasn't my fault that I was expected to hook up with David, because he was an available biological male who wasn't creepy in the 27 year old hippie circle I hung out in. Yes, David was 27 too. Is this what you get when you drop outta college?

When we arrived at the beach on the coast, next to RV's and families in campers, Colin smiled and took out a little tincture bottle. "This here," he snickered, "is 100% pure lsd. You can't get this anywhere. This is rare." Everybody stuck out their tongues as Colin placed a little drop on them. When it came to be my turn, I stuck my tongue out, trying to act all tough and macho as if I had done lsd before. But I hadn't and I was scared shitless, especially drops of strong pure acid. I guess I was still kinda Natasha's fake-girlfriend cuz I took that LSD drop for her (and my own personal spiritual purposes as well, duh) and tried to act all tough and macho, to prove something to her. Not the butt-rock hippie boys. I didn't care about them. But, I was still scared shitless, wondering what in the hell this drug was going to do to me, this time. This was that phase in life that you'd classify as: experimental as all hell soul searcher will take any drug that moves.

Colin, Dave, Natasha and I all took a long stroll on the beach. Nastasha whispered to me "you're so cool." I knew she was saying that, cuz I went and took the drug. We watched the sunset, made sandcastles, and waited for the drugs to hit. An I-drank-too-much-coffee type of pain erupted in my stomach, and soon enough I had loads of energy. Was this what taking lsd was like? After the beach, we all decided to walk around the small coastal town, eventually finding a playground to play on. This is where the drugs really hit me. I was lost. I was dazed and confused, but not like the movie, I was the real dazed and confused. I couldn't figure out how to get to the slide Colin was going down on, *cuz there were weird yellow things in the way. did the weird yellow things exist? And what In the hell are weird yellow things?* I ran up to David and asked if he could hold my hand so I couldn't get lost. He reluctantly did so. "David" I yelled "I'm fucking tripping outta my mind. Please fucking hold my hand." David clenched me, and we all walked back to the beach. Dogs began to chase us with their loud, obnoxious barking. But I think I was having some "lsd realization" cuz the barking didn't annoy me or scare me like they usually do. The dogs just needed more love is what I thought. Man, was I tripping. Lsd and street smarts do not mix well with this so called urban hermitt. Once back at the beach, the sand was erupting into mini volcanoes. Out in the ocean, secret ancient Egyptian messages were being typed out by the stars. The moon was moving at fast speed. And I couldn't move past the sand volcanoes without getting lost. Of course, no one else was seeing this, and they were all laughing at me.

I tried to explain the secrets of the universe to everybody as they sat on a log and smoked pot. "It's like every step you take" I professed "can be a step into a new dimension. Reality is that intense dude!"

"Hermitt, what the fuck are you talking about?" Natasha laughed. Nobody got it, they were all poking fun at me when all I was trying to do was FIGURE IT ALL OUT. But, dear reader, I am sober as can be as I write this down right now, and I sure as hell assure you that I still believe that every step you take can take you into a different state of consciousness. It's not hard to understand. Just use your imagination. This is when I decided that all my friends were fucking stupid and treated lsd like a party drug. I was on some vision guru quest and they were out for a good time. I stopped ranting my philosophical jargon and began to listen to them.

Colin: "Oh smooshy lips, aren't the colors funny?"

Natasha: "Tee Hee oh yes... hee hee hee."

David: "let's smoke some pot!"

Hermitt: "what does it all mean?"

The greatest thing I've ever learned on lsd: not everybody is trying to figure it out like me. All my friends were annoying me, so I just looked away and tripped out on everything. I saw a lady light up a cigarette in the distance, I could see the red cigarette light go inside her body. I could see her kidneys. When I closed my eyes, though, all I saw were japanese animation cartoon characters. Then I decided to hug everybody, when I hugged them, I saw dancing grateful dead bears. Bears everywhere. Funny, my drug trip was turning into a grateful dead tee shirt. It made sense, it's just that it was just plain ridiculous.

Eventually, everybody set out for bed. Colin and Natasha in the tent. David and I in the van. I knew we weren't going to hook up. I just stared at the ceiling, watching Marilyn Monroe turn into different kinds of Andy Warhol art, while David slept peacefully. When I woke up, I was still tripping. I wasn't seeing any bears or volcanoes, or japanese animation cartoon creatures. I just wanted to breathe, watch the ocean waves, and drink a cup of water: The simple things. Simple things, however, weren't good enough for Natasha, who woke me up early. "did he do you?" she maliciously asked.

"No, he didn't do me!" I snapped back.

"Hermitt, when are you going to get it on? You need a man!" she snapped back, even harder. I was silent. I didn't respond. I couldn't talk. I just wanted to go home and read my holy books and maybe Jane would show up, and my life would make sense. Colin and David woke up, drank the rest of the franzia boxed wine, and we drove back to the Big City. En route to the Big City, we stopped in a small town for food. While I prompted for the local supermarket, everybody else prompted for fucking mcdonald's. I protested and protested as much as I could, but to no avail, David parked his big red van in the McDonald's parking lot. They all ordered Big Macs, while I ate a muffin wondering why in the hell I had to be in mcdonald's after an intense-spiritual drug trip. *But Hermitt* my brain said *These people aren't trying to figure it all out like you, so why would they be conscious now if they weren't conscious then?* I thanked my brain and growled at my friends. My brain didn't know everything, but it sure as hell knowed that mcdonald's is not real food and lsd isn't just a party.

I didn't talk to anybody for the rest of the ride back to The Big City. Yes, I was being snooty. That's ok, though, I love The Smiths, Thrift Store Clothing, Coffeeshops, and Zines that are actually good, that equals a snooty person you know. I was mildly proud of that. David dropped me off at the urban communal hippie house. They were gone and here I was. No one was home. I decided to get some perspective on what had all just happened. I picked up the tattered "Love Under Will" book (aka: The Holy Book) for a second time. I was hurting for some spiritual advice. I threw some granola in some yogurt, and sat my ass down on a living room chair and began to read. I recited out loud, in my head, what the book was telling me to do.

Yes, oh holy book. I am a divine being.

Yes, oh holy book, I will try not to drink or do drugs anymore. Because if I do that, I'll be closer to spiritual bliss even though, oh Holy Book, I am a fat ass hypocrite and will probably drink or smoke pot tonite. But reading this Holy Book is at least a start?

Star, during all of this nonsense, was sitting across from me, chatting away in fast fluent Spanish on the phone. She kept winking at me, but I couldn't let her distract me. The book was calling.

Yes, oh Holy Book, I know that I have the power to be a healer but is it okay that I really

97

like to sit around, mope, and listen to The Smiths and Joy Division? Can that be considered healing as well?

Holy Book, you say that "god" has transmuted you special messages, does that mean that I can receive these messages from "god" as well?

I turned the page and The Holy Book told me, that no, although I am *a healer and a child of light and love,* that I could not receive these special messages from "god." I was a bit bummed, but now, more encouraged than ever to go out and do more drugs! Star gets off the telephone, stares at the "Love Under Will" book and exudes a freaked out look on her face. "wow Hermitt, you're reading that book!"

"Yeah, well" I explain "I'm reading it for the second time, it's kinda interesting, but kinda preachy."

"Wow! That's what Jane said too! She's reading that book for the second time too. That's sooooooo trippy dude" Star shouts.

"Uh" is all that I have to say. Star laughs a bit, gets up, and leaves. Right now, I am wondering if Jane, wherever she may be, is having conversations in her head with this Holy Book like I am. I know that right now there are tons of kids doing drugs, seeing things, eating at mcdonald's, and trying to figure it all out. But right now, I don't know about this Jane thing.

THIS LETTER SAYS THAT I AM IN BIG TROUBLE!

Dear Urban Hermitt,

This letter serves as a Notice. This is an attempt to collect you from your Rigid-Gender-Roles debt. Submitting into a societially desired female gender role now, will help you get out of the serious debt you have gotten yourself into, young lady. We at the National Council for Rigid Gender Roles understand that you may not be able to directly pay all your gender debt at once, that is why we can offer you payment plans in 17 monthly installments.

First Month: Start Shaving your legs (only with the pink razors that we have designed for you) and grow your hair out. (no dreadlocks and no mullets allowed.)

Second Month: Let every man you meet always open doors for you. Laugh at every joke he says, and let him carry things for you. This is, of course, for your best interest. All Males are born stronger than females. That is just the way things work around here.

Third Month: Start a diet of low fat cottage cheese, melba toast, and Diet Coke with lemon.

Fourth Month: Start making comments like "Oh you silly boys" or "oh let's give the rest of the food to the boys so that they can grow to be big and strong!" The more and more you make these strategic comments, the more smooth your credit report will be. And as a reward for sticking with us for four months, we will present you a pink embodied credit card to the women's section at Banana Republic clothing stores.

Fifth Month: Repeat everything we have told you to do, and you will be out of debt in 12 months.

You have 30 days to respond to our Notice, and start making your payment plans. Enclosed is the latest edition of The Oprah Magazine and a copy of a book written by Dr. Laura.

Kd Lang is Dead,
Wolfe Miette
Chief Consumer Reporter
The National Council for Rigid Gender Roles
Dallas, Texas

12."DANK PRODUCTIONS" IS AT IT AGAIN!

I was sitting at the vegan café that served nasty tasty food, but I still ate there anyway, because it was a local restaurant, I was pretending to be vegan, and I was really into supporting local restaurants as an opposition to eating at Mcdonald's. Adding large amounts of salt to my vegan biscuits and gravy, a simple man in blue jeans, white tee shirt, and black converse all star high tops came up and sat down next to me. He introduced himself as Samuel Cowens, and told me that he was really into drawing cartoons. I told him that I was really into "trying to figure it all out." We got to talking, and I found out that Samuel used to be a businessman in Los Angeles before he adopted his current life of blue jeans, cartoon drawing, and hanging out at the vegan café all day long. "Just, what kind of businessman were you?" I asked.

"Oh you know, I dealt with media and the such." Samuel said, trying to beat around the bush.

"Oh, what kind of media Samuel?" suspiciously, I asked, wondering if he was part of some drug cartel. And it was at that, Samuel began to explain to me that he was a businessman for DANK PRODUCTIONS. DANK PRODUCTIONS was responsible for designing 300 dollar bongs, 30 dollar tee shirts that said 4:20, and various pro-marijuana raves all around the country. "I guess you could say that I was a hippie businessman, except in a slimy way" he added on. Immediately, I was fascinated by this, since not only was I getting hate mail from slimly hippie businessmen, but I was beginning to brew conspiracy theories that businessmen in Los Angeles were trying to make a market on the hippie culture. I asked Samuel if I could do an interview, and he agreed. Things were getting spicy.

Hermitt: So how did you become to be a hippie businessman?

Samuel: Well, it was back in the late 80's, I had just finished following the Grateful Dead around the country. I had been doing that since I graduated from high school. Well, while following the Dead, I ended up hooking up with a beautiful lady, and she got pregnant. She decided to keep the baby, so we moved in with her parents in LA, while I looked for work to support everybody. At the time, I had long dreadlocks, and looked like I had just walked out of a Rainbow Gathering, so I didn't know who in the hell was going to hire me. All morning I'd roll around town, filling out applications. In the afternoon, I'd head out to Venice Beach to surf a bit. I was having bad luck finding a job until one day I was out in the water waiting to catch a wave. I met this guy, another surfer, who seemed very curious about my life. After I told him that I just got back from following The Grateful Dead, he offered me a job as a "managing marketer" at a new business firm called DANK PRODUCTIONS. At the time, I didn't seriously believe that he was offering me a job on the spot while we were surfing, but when I went in the next day to the DANK PRODUCTIONS office, I had a job.

Hermitt: What exactly is a hippie businessman and what was this DANK PRODUCTIONS all about? And didn't the slang word "dank" not come out until the 90's?

Samuel: It's hard to exactly say what a hippie businessman is. However, I was told that I was hired to seek out what was hip in the hippie market range.

Hermitt: What is a hippie market range?

Samuel: A hippie market range is what people in a certain hippie culture will buy, whether it be the hippies who are into the Dead, the hippies who are into auras/new age, or the hippies who are into drugs. So I guess, a hippie businessman caters to that. The dudes behind Ben and Jerry's Ice Cream are kind of like hippie businessmen, they have ice cream flavors named after famous hippie bands like The Grateful Dead and Phish. (IE: Cherry Garcia Ice Cream and Phish Food Ice Cream) DANK PRODUCTIONS, in my opinion was really all about the money. They didn't really care if their market range was hippies, Jehovah

Witness, gun totting hillbillies, or any of that. They just knew that a lot of hippies had money, like the kids who were raised wealthy, and like hippie culture because it looks cool, and today's yuppies who used to be hippies in the 60's. You would think that most hippies are poor, but think otherwise. They just hired me cuz they knew I could tell them what would sell. I didn't care, I needed the money. And about the word DANK, well I really don't know where it came from or originated from. but I can tell you this: the word HELLA originated in the late 80's in Los Angeles, and that's a fact.

Hermitt: Do you think such a concept as hippie market range, contradicts all the things the original hippies were down for?

Samuel: Of course it does. But is there such thing as an original hippie anymore? Don't you think that kids these days, like yourself, do I might say, turn to hippie culture as a result of the way it has been displayed in the mass media? There are tv shows about hippies, movies, ice cream flavors, etc... Tim Leary is a household name. The Black Crowes and Sublime are all over MTV. You young hippie kids may think that you are not influenced by mainstream society at all, but you are. In fact, even the hippies of the 60's were influenced by mainstream society as well.

Hermitt: But didn't you feel bad that you were helping to milk money outta young innocent kids who were trying hippie stuff out so that they could figure life out?

Samuel: Should I? Obviously if they are buying our stuff, then they are not soul searchers, they are consumers. They think they are hippies, but if they sat down and did the research, they would see that there is more to life. But believe me, I was fooled too. When I was following the Grateful Dead and selling mushrooms outside the shows, I thought that I was so radical and living the perfect hippie life. My opinion changed greatly when I started working for DANK PRODUCTIONS. I found out that the tie dye tee shirts with dancing Grateful Dead bears on them that I had been wearing, were made in sweatshops in Honduras. I found out that the weed I was smoking was actually grown in government regulated universities. So I sat down and did the research. It took me to be a fucking businessman in Los Angeles, to finally figure out what was going on. I found out that ancient shaman never sold mushrooms, and advised others not too, because it was ruining the sacredness of the plant. That was deeper than any Grateful Dead song ever written. So I stopped selling drugs, joined a Mushroom Enthusiast Society, and picked the damn things myself.

Hermitt: Do you think businesses like DANK PRODUCTIONS mind warp people?

Samuel: Well, I don't think they subliminally tell people to believe in the government or become a television evangelist. However, I do think they contribute to the mass consumerism in this society. Kids these days actually spend money on drugs and pipes! They spend money on their clothes and music! That's just the same as anybody else. Current hippie culture has nothing to do with peace, love, and happiness. It was to do with a mass market of people trying to make money and playing off the weak who can't think for themselves. That goes for any subculture as well.

Hermitt: That's kind of harsh, Samuel. What about mass rad things like locally owned natural food co-ops, cafes, and collectives? What about the people who make their own herbal tinctures, knitted caps, and instruments?

Samuel: That's not hippie. That's community and rad people working together towards social change. Not everybody who goes to a natural foods co-op is a hippie. That's why eventually I left DANK PRODUCTIONS and Los Angeles all together. My girlfriend left me a few years earlier, and took our daughter with her. So I moved up here, started to work at a natural food's co-op, joined a bike collective, returned to my passion of drawing comics, and just got real.

Hermitt: What does getting real mean?

Samuel: Oh, you can't describe it. Let me just say that *Punk Rock is more than the Ramones and Hip Hop is more than Public Enemy.*

Hermitt: Did you come up with that statement yourself?

Samusl: No, I read it on a sticker done by Microcosm Publishing and it inspired me. I don't really listen to much punk or hip hop, but I occasionally listen to some Public Enemy.

Hermitt: Cool!

LOOK! JUNK MAIL:

Dear Urban Hermitt,

Have you tried the latest hemp-granola seed rasta energy bar? Well, if you have, then you have experienced the quality and expertise that is associated with DANK PRODUCTIONS. What is DANK PRODUCTIONS, you may ask? Well, we only serve the finest in rasta-hemp products. Our new fall line features Bob Marley lollipops, Hemp Hair gel (for all those growing dreadlocks out there!), multi-colored dance pants from Guatemala, hemp nut seed condoms with rasta colors on them, wildcrafted nettle fiber kitchen scrubbies (of course, made with 25% hemp seed extract), Maui Waui Essential Oil (for all the ladies out there, this is a great alternative to patchouli oil), and our new honey coated "make your own dreadlocks at home" wax for kids! Yes, as you can see, we cater to all the "brothers" and "sisters." And coming soon, in January, experience our multi faith audio mediation guides, come experience the inner peace gained by our multi faith audio guides. And with purchases of 2 or more, you will receive a FREE, complementary set of multi faith cotton embodied 100% organic soy ink based prayer flags!

DANK PRODUCTIONS started back in the heart of Los Angeles, when in 1986, local entrepreneur Ezkiel CottonFlower just returned from a pilgrimage to the World International Rainbow Gathering in Brazil! At the World International Rainbow Gathering, Ezekiel saw that vendors were promoting their hemp rasta products from all over the world, yet he was not seeing any of this in Los Angeles. Ezekiel had to represent his people. "Why has it taken me to trek all the way down to Brazil to realize that I am neglecting my own people?" he humbly thought to himself. With that, he started DANK PRODUCTIONS, set up an office in West Hollywood, started tie dying Jimi Hendrix Hooded Sweatshirts, and started sending "scouts" to go to all The Grateful Dead Shows in the nation, to find out what the people want. Or as John Lennon said "Power to the People, right on!"

We hope that you will choose to be an intelligent consumer and choose DANK PRODUCTIONS the next time you make a purchase. We accept Visa, Mastercard, and American Express.

Namaste,
Ezkiel CottonFlower
Founder of DANK PRODUCTIONS
Los Angeles, California

13. JANE'S ADDICTION:

A touring Grateful Dead cover band from Arizona had taken over the urban hippie communal house. Four guitar players, a drummer, the dreddy girlfriend who made hemp necklaces in the backyard, and a smiley chubby bear-like dude who sat wisely in the living room. "So, what do you do in the band?" I asked, on a sunny spring day. "Well" he smiled "I'm the band's personal astrologer." He said this in a calm, nonchalant manner as if every touring band has a personal astrologer.

"And what is your name?" he kindly asked

"Hermitt."

"Well Hermitt, what is your sign?"

"I'm a Taurus." I said. I gatta tell you though, at this point I was paranoid and hella scared that Mr. Astrologer was going start telling me how much I was like Jane because I am a Taurus.

"Well Hermitt, do you know what your other signs are?"

"Other signs?" I said, confused but sure as hell happy that he didn't even mentioned the name Jane.

"Yeah, like your Moon sign, and Pluto, Venus etc."

"What... in... the... hell... does... that all mean?"

"Well, when you're born, your sun sign is determined by where the sun is. So your other signs mean, where was the moon positioned when you were born? Where was Pluto? Astrology is way more than your sun sign," he said, so wisely. This guy was cool. He handed me a stack of books about all of this, and encouraged me to study this new found knowledge. I thanked him for the books, he closed his eyes and meditated, and I went into my room to continue my studies on figuring it all out. I decided to say goodbye to the Holy Books, and learn practical, rational things. I studied charts and lists. What I came out with was that almost every planet of mine is Taurus. I was being stalked by my own personal astrology. To top it of, it was now the month of May. May is the month Tauruses are born.

If things couldn't get topped off anymore, outside in the backyard I heard the words "Jane! Hey, it's you! Welcome home Jane!" right as I realized that I am a quadropile Taurus. Was that really Jane in the backyard? I turned my head, and there was a tall Latino babe with a shaved head, and thick toned muscles standing at my door, staring right at me. Could it be? She was gorgeous and a dyke! My pants got hella wet and I said my trademarked words of "Uh... hi."

"Yo! I didn't mean to bother you or anything. My name's Jane. This used to be my room. I... I... I just wanted to check the room out and see who was living in it."

"Uh... hi" I said so nervously "My name's Hermitt."

"Hi Hermitt. Well, it was nice meeting you, I should let you be" At that, Jane was gone. I was stunned, standing there in all horror. I obviously was not a tall latino babe in a shaved head. I was more like a short-of-european-descent-dork-in-dreadlocks. All rational thought was lost, and my ego stepped in. I took out my skateboard deck, walked past Jane chatting away in fast fluent Spanish in the living room with Star, and jetted on outside to skate on a clear May day. I figured if Jane knew that I skated, it would make me look more tough and studly. Even though I was still having a hard time admitting to myself that I needed pussy bad, and I could smell her sweet fruity pussy juices a mile away. (Keep in mind, girls skateboarding circa 1996-1997 was not a popular thing , Nowadays, more and more girls seem to skate. But back then, it was a big fucking deal if you were a girl and skateboarded. Yeah I know you're laughing, dear reader, thinking that I'm making 1996 sound like it was a long time ago. But it was long enough ago for things to change.)

When I got back from my skateboarding adventures, I walked through the basement door only to find Jane shaving her head. "Hey Hermitt, can you help me shave the back of my head to make sure it's even" she said. I agreed and shaved the back of her head. It was pure torture, touching her back, shoulders, scalp, and sweet head. It was the most flirtatious thing anybody could do to you. I even shaved when I didn't need to shave just so I could touch her more. The more I touched, the more I got wet, and the more I didn't understand how in the hell I was like Jane. I got scared, put the razor down, and ran up to my room to hide. Hiding in my room though, I blasted cool hip hop as a secret attempt to show off to Jane more. It was a music battle, cuz then Jane blasted Ani Difranco really loud down there in the basement. It was the newly released Ani Difranco live album "Living in Clip." Perhaps her last great album, and a milestone in time for dyke culture? Well, at the time I was not dyke culture, and it was the first time I ever heard Ani DiFranco. Aha! So that's what she sounds like I thought, I always hearing stories of how leeezbuins listen to Ani DiFranco, which isn't true, but I thought was true when the world was a lot more young. Ego-wise, I still kept the hip hop on, but I was secretly putting my ear against the floor to hear what this Ani DiFranco sounded like. I could also hear Jane sing along to the tunes, in this really cheesy jazz voice that was turning me on nonetheless. I sat down, listened to folk music verse hip hop, and wrote love poetry.

The next day I decided that I was going to go perform my newly inspired love poetry at the local open mic at the vegan café. I wasn't trying to prove anything to anybody with the poetry, I was just sprung! I sat in my room all day, practicing. My bitter roommate even bought me wine because she told me that reading at an open mic for the first time is really liberating. I went downstairs to the basement to see what was up. Randy was making candles. Jane was napping. I chatted away with Randy. Jane, then, got up from her nap and was immediately in my face asking "So Hermit, what are you doing tonite?"

"Oh, um... uh, I'm reading poetry at an open mic."

"Cool! Can I come?" she smiled. This was pure torture.

"Sure."

Jane said that she would meet me there since she had "shit to do." I was hella nervous. But I sucked it all in, grabbed my scattered poetry papers, and headed off to the vegan café. My heart was beating faster than all the drugs my little body could take. (I started taking Hawthorne Berry extract, due to my heart beating so fast from being hella nervous all the time. Hawthorne Berries are good for your heart, all you hard core coffee drinkers out there.) At the café, everybody seemed so much more hip, older, and in the know. I didn't say a word to anybody, put my name on the sign up list, and

114

bought a brownie. Slowly, I ate crumb by crumb of the brownie, staring at the tall hippie men in goatees and Guatemalan pants. The little old ladies in grey sweaters drinking tea. The kids in their mid twenties dressed like swank swing kids. Who was I? A stone butch dyke disguised as a hippie? Was the disguise even working?

Jane showed up. Immediately, she sat down at my table, and grabbed my hands, slowly touching and caressing them. Shit dude I thought we are holding hands like they did in that awesome dyke movie "The Incredibly True Adventures of Two Girls in Love" this is so trippy. We caressed hands and played footsie. Jane winked. "Yo man" she said, then paused for a bit as if she were trying to look cool "I was walking around this town today, and I was thinking... I was thinking about you. I was thinking about how cool you are." I blushed and then, as reality has it, it was my time to read at the open mic.

And then I thought *shit dude, now this is so not like that awesome dyke movie "The Incredibly True Adventures of Two Girls in Love."*

"Up next, we have Hermitt, who has never read here before. Let's give it up for Hermitt" the host said. I almost tripped on myself walking up there. Everything was in slow motion. Jane was staring at me and of course I couldn't read my love poetry about her. That would be too embarrassing. So I read my awful drug poetry and fucked up. Drug poetry is the worst poetry

115

out there simply because when you are on The Drugs you may think that your poetry is so good but when you read it to people who are Off The Drugs, they may think otherwise. The audience barely clapped. But that was totally ok, cuz I go back to the table, Jane grabs my hand some more and says "Let's get some beer, I just turned 21 last week." I didn't need poetry, I needed a good time. Plus, over 21 year olds buying me booze was the bonus of my life.

We walk to the store together. This is when I realize that we are walking the same, wearing our backpacks the same, and even moving our hands the same. Can you say identity crisis? Jane and I browse the beer aisle at the local supermarket and decide on the most lesbionic beer you can think of: apricot beer! If apricot beer right now is not the current favorite brew of the dykes, then it will be. Why? Because Pussy tastes like fruit, but fruit that's not too sweet. Pussy tastes like apricot and has the same texture as apricot. Dykes are not fruity people, they just taste good (except all the evil bitches who have broke my poor heart). Hence, the apricot beer. Not lemon. Not stout. Not beach. Not any wicked summer, fall, or winter brew.

Back at the hippie house, everybody is freaking out. Julie shouts "Jane, where have you been?" Star adds in "Jane, we were worried about you." Nobody was worried about me. They don't even say Hello. "I was at a poetry reading with Hermitt" Jane announces. All the hippies are surprised thus making the whole moment very awkward. Jane

116

comes up and whispers in my ear "Hermitt, what do you do when you get bored?"

"I skateboard."

"Let's take these beers and go skating."

"But I only have one skateboard."

"Who cares" Jane says like a true champ, "but I know where I can get another one." She runs upstairs without a word. A few minutes later, she comes down with a thick early 1980's deck with Death Metal drawings on the bottom... We put the beers in our matching backpacks and hit the streets. Outside a university, I bump into this kid who I hadn't seen in a long long long time meaning that I went to grade school with him. Was it cosmic or was reality fucking with me? He asks me how I am doing and I wish I could have said that I was about to come out as a dyke. But instead, I make up some bullshit answer and catch up with Jane. We take a break from skating and sit next to a fountain, and mini-chapel on the university campus. We are sitting very far apart from each other. I drop my beer. The glass breaks everywhere. And then Jane asks me the question?

"So do you like guys or girls or guys and girls? What is it Hermitt?"

"Uh... Uh... " and then I said the most bullshit-hippie-dippie-answer I could think of "Uh, well Jane, I think I just like people, you know? What about you?"

117

"Well I had this girlfriend once but she hurt me really bad." That was Jane's response. To be nice, I went and hugged her. This scared Jane and she jumped up. "Hey Hermitt! Let's try to ring the church bell!" she yelled. Soon enough I was chasing Jane up a long church bell tower, pushing her up and touching her tight ass. We were rubbing and rubbing, all the way up to the bell. *Hermitt, you're gay! you're gay! You're gay!* my brain told me, and I agreed. Jane probably agreed too, except that I was touching her ass a bit too friendly which prompted Jane to slide down the church bell tower and announce that maybe we should be leaving now, so we won't get caught. We skated back to the hippie house and didn't say a word to each other for the rest of the night. I fell asleep with a big smile on my face. It didn't really matter if I had kissed Jane or not, as long as I was coming true with myself.

A few days later Jane left. We didn't hang out much the last few days she was in The Big City. Right before she left for the airport, she came into my room, grabbed my hands, and told me that we would see each other again. The next day I left for the Rainbow Gathering: another attempt to figure it all out.

GOOD BEER LETTER:

Dear Urban Hermitt,

Thank you for writing about how you love to drink apricot beer. Not only is it a good tasting beverage, it is also the beer of dyke champions! Not any ol' dykes but dykes who are champions! Apricot beer will not be found on tap at the local cheezy lesbian bar, NO! Apricot beer will be found, however, on back porches where good friends hang out. Apricot beer will be found in your room as Tricky's "Maxinquaye" album plays and you try to get your groove on with a feisty sexy young dyke thang. You will not find this pussy-tasting beer on billboard commercials, becuz it is the underground beer of dyke champions! The question is, Urban Hermitt, do you think that there is another beer out there that tastes like pussy? If so, I hope that it is not lemon beer. Lemon beer is for wimps! Besides beer, I have found that Annie's Natural Goddess Salad Dressing, Baked Ginger Tofu, Stirfry, and Grilled Cheeze Sandwiches all taste like Pussy. My Pussy tastes like Stirfry with tempeh, broccoli, garlic, ginger, and cilantro. What does yours taste like?

Your Fan,
Korey Duker
Atlanta, GA

14. THE RAINBOW GATHERING MADE ME GAY, GIRLFRIEND!

Like the good little save-the-earthers we are, Tracy and I sit on a log eating oatmeal slop outta reusable mugs full of political stickers. Oatmeal slop is the only thing that is served at the Rainbow Gathering. Ooops, I mean The 1997 National Rainbow Gathering Of Living Love and Light. Whatever that means. The Rainbow Gathering is the Rainbow Gathering and *Oatmeal Slop is at least 5lbs of cheap oats usually originating from the food bank or the bottom shelf at safeway/mega-power-save-on-whatever-foods mixed with cinnamon and apples.* But I sure as hell wasn't complaining, here I was eating food for free under a shinning sun next to a sweet-smiling' Tracy watching middle aged hippie men in the nude chase their 5 year old kids in dreadlocks chasing their golden retriever dogs named after all Bob Marley songs written after the year 1976. Names such as "Kaya" "Exodus" etc...

As I sit on the humble little log deep in the heart of The Oregon National Forest, a girl with a third eye sticker on her forehead comes up to me, in all utter franticness, and loudly exclaimed that "at this moment in time I am seeing The Truth!" I tell her that I don't believe her since I have just realized that every person on this goddamned planet think that they are Right and will go to the ends of the earth to convince you of this. Tears flow outta this girls eyes, I try to apologize, but then she jumps up and starts dancing to the neverending beat of the drum circle. The drum circle sounds are everywhere. At every camp fire and kitchen and tent area, big large burly men who really look like Conan the Barbarian with uber long beards are pounding away towards something, maybe the living loving light of some rainbow that I sure as hell don't feel apart of. Well, I do feel connected to Tracy. Even though I just met her yesterday in a van, on the way to the Rainbow Gathering. So I try not to judge the lady with the third eye sticker who tries to convince me of "the way." Instead, I grab Tracy and convince her to start roaming around with me to look for something interesting.

We tromp onto the Main Path with our packs on. Immediately, every single person we walk past starts saying "WELCOME HOME SEEEEEEESTER..." as if we have just arrived 5 minutes ago. "I'm already fuckn' home fuckn' arrrgh" I mumble underneath my breath. I was trying to feel the "love" and join Tracy with her perma-grin-smile-of-what-appears-to-be-love. But the majik wasn't happening. "Look" Tracy says in midst if my own personal doomed-thought process "there's two hella fine guys sitting on the side of the trail." I look over only to see two scraggly 18-year-old-ish dudes with white-people-red-haired afros holding up a pipe connecting to a pole and some string. Like a fishing pole. Underneath, there was a sign that said "will fish for weed." And "got 4:20?" This was during that late 1990's craze of "got milk?" and "got pot?" tee shirt/commercial advertising frenzy. (See DANK PRODUCTIONS for more information on this topic.) "It's so creative" Tracy gleed. "Right On!" I gleed back, all the while secretly harboring more complex thoughts about why the hippie men looked more like me than the hippie women yet everybody kept calling me "Hey Sister" as if this was the right thing to do. I was secretly jealous of all the hippie men who wanted to fuck me. The only reason I was a hippie mama babe at the time, was that I let my big tits hang, sported thick dreadlocks, and wore patchouli with great intensity. I even put patchouli on the hair above and around the hair that complements my vaginal regions AkA: THE BUSH. The bitter yet aromatic smells of the patchouli squeezed between my wet-oh-tracy-I-secretly-want-you thighs and seeped into the same air the hippie men breathed. It was getting to be a bit to much. I was waiting for a dog or a faerie fag who only sucked dick, to come save Tracy and I from the penetrative obsessed breeders. Then... a miracle arises! No faerie fags, but a wooden sign that said "kids camp." Kids rule! And kids aren't creepy men who only wanna fuck you cuz some DNA chromosomes gave you a pussy.

The Kid's Camp was a couple of tipis and a couple of hippie moms chasing little young ones. Cedar Sunlight come back here and finish your oatmeal! Sakoya Hazelweed come back here and give Lazarus his beanie back! Moses Ezkiel would you like to smell some lavender essential oil on mommy's tit? It was really sweet. The kids seemed so untouched and pure. They didn't even seem hippie at all even though their parents gave them the names and dressed them in the clothes. That's what makes kids... kids. 21 year olds, 46 year olds can be kids too, you just probably won't meet that many during your time here on The Human Centric Planet. And that's ok. It ain't your fault.

Tracy and I sat down on a log and watched the kids dance and run around making silly noises like "ooooooooooooopks-burg-faaaaa-faaaaa-foo!" During this joy, a girl comes up to us and starts playing the flute. Her songs sounded like the backdrop for a northern French medieval fest and not a rainbow gathering. It was all LA LA. But that joyous LA LA does not sound interesting on paper, Dear Reader, so I'll spare you the bad-yet-positive-poetry and move on to the point when the girl stopped playing the flute and started chatting it up with Tracy and I.

"Hi, my name's Sky."

"Hermitt." I stared into her deep blue eyes and wondered if she liked girls and I really like girls or if I only like girls and she knew

123

this and it scared her or if she was the one who like girls and I was a liking girls poseur due to my jealousy issues with the hippie men.

"Well Hermitt, it's nice to be here, isn't it?"

"Oh Yes" I half assed said.

Sky didn't seem that hippie. She seemed more KID even though contemporary social thought and governmental papers would classify her as ADULT. She wore nothing but a holey tee-shit and torn up jeans and had that mid-curly-hair-doo where it's not really a hair-doo, it just looks like somebody is trying to grow their curly hair out. I began to ask Sky things like "so where do you come from?" and to which she said "Oh, you know... I'm from around like Mt. Shasta, but I really don't know what I am doing, the only thing I own in the world is this here spoon and bowl that a lady gave to me here. I was in Mt. Shasta and this guy asks me if I want to hitch to the Rainbow Gathering with him, so I said why not? So tell me about yourself Hermitt."

Oh, I felt so embarrassed to share myself with her. My life seemed so conservative and trapped compared to her *free-owning-nothing-I-live-in-mt. shasta-life*. Mt Shasta is a pretty intense spiritual place whereas The Big City is, like, a pretty city that ruins itself by trying to be a baby San Francisco. And so I respond to Sky by saying "Well, you know. I live in a house, work at a pizza place, and skate, and shit." I

124

purposely left out "I am an in the closet lesbo" and "I am a pot-head-lazy-ass." But Sky gave me a big hug, told me I was sincerely beautiful, and said that she would love to stay but she is about to leave to go hitchhike somewhere else with somebody else. Ten seconds later... Sky is gone. It's just me and Tracy.

After Sky left, there didn't seem like there was anymore purpose left in the kid's camp. Tracy and I strapped on our dirty blue jansport backpacks and trekked back to the main road. What would usually be an easy, mild mid day trek back to the main road, was accosted and highly interrupted by a swarm of kids marching on thru. They were banging pots and pans all the while screaming some loud gibberish that would be deemed as "cute" by those who chose to identify as ADULT and not KID. Leading the pack of screaming pseudo-marching band kids was a tall man who looked like santa claus after about 5 pints of guinness, shouting "please donate money in this bin so that we can get money to get the kids ice cream. Get the kids ice cream!" Behind Mr. Santa Claus, all the little kids yelled "ice creweanmmmm ice... cereheeeeweeeeeem!" as if topics such as "sugar addiction" and "A.D.D." and "bratty child syndrome" existed all too well the at 1997 National Rainbow Gathering of Living Love and Light. After I saw the last lil' rainbow kid, I thought that the parade was all done, but then an entire posse of earth mamma hippies in homemade sweaters/patchwork dresses followed the parade all the while screaming "give the kids ice cream! Give the kids ice cream!"

Intense... but not cult like. I didn't give any money cuz I was still a kid and I wanted somebody to buy me ice cream too. You know? Oh well. The parade is over, and tracy and I got some crazy mad wandering to do. This place is huge. Not only is it in a massive grand national forest, there are literally 50,000 hippies in the woods at once, all either on a) the drugs b) the new age c) the soul seeker d) the kids who got dragged here. Well, gosh dolley, I am category #c and I sure as hell gatta meet mo' soul seekers here. I look around in a sea of jesus lookin hippies (I'm not kidding here when I say that almost everybody at the Rainbow Gathering looks like jesus. I mean the christian white lookin jesus that a lotta people are brainwashed to believe in. cuz jesus was probably brown and I can assure you that there ain't too many brown peeps at this rainbow fest. This is for real. And lest, I have to remind you that this book, THE URBAN HERMITT, is not fiction, it is creative non-fiction therefore the statement: most people at the rainbow gathering really do look like jesus is... kinda... like... true!) and don't really feel out the soul seeker vibe. I hold onto tracy's hand and start to get really confused. Thoughts start to cloud mee wee lil' head:

Is this what woodstock was really like?

When my mom did things in the 60s. was it like this?

If I took more acid, would I connect with

everybody and actually understand this Rainbow
Gathering Love Light Whatever Gig?
Does Tracy get off when she touches me too?

What does pussy taste like and when I get
there, will I actually like it?

In the midst of all this, a tiny girl in dirty
blond dreadlocks runs past me screaming. She
stops and yells to the sky: "whoa shit dude, this
is crazy... man... where did you guys go... whoa...
these mushrooms are crazy maaaaan... fuck you
guys all of you... whoa..." Tracy laughs. I get
scared to ever eat mushrooms again. Then the
dirty blond dready girl starts walking in circles
and hitting things. a burly man in a tie dye tee
shirt comes up to her, pats her on the back and
says "calm down sister... calm down." Following
the man in the tie dye tee shirt, are about 30
other people in tie dye tee shirts who come up
to tell the girl trippin' out on mushrooms to
"calm down." They were saying "calm down" so
frantically that they weren't even "calm downed."

Well, I'm not calm, man. There is too much
happening at once. This is worse than the city.
My heart is a thump a thump-thumping. I ran out
of my natural Hawthorne Berry drops to de-thump
thump my heart, so things were fucked. Tracy is
smiling like the rainbow master came down and
saved her. The girl on mushrooms is still hitting
everybody. But then, out of the blue, a loud bell
rings. The bell keeps on ringing as if it is
important. Tracy informs me that this is the

"universal diner bell." Universal dinner bell? "oh, that means that everybody goes up to the main field to eat a communal dinner." Within 4 seconds of discovering this knowledge, I grab Tracy by the belly, and run towards this field of FOOD. Saved by the bell and saved by the food.

Funny, the communal dinner was more like a stadium size dinner. There were at least 3000 people sitting down on the grass in a big circle. All the people just sat and sat, until three men in brown dreadlocks got into the middle of the circle and started talking. "Welcome... brothers and sisters," they yelled "before we eat, we need to make a few announcements. First off, a few hours ago, there was a kind sister who was having a bad experience on mushrooms. Her friends had left her. That was not kind. I repeat... that was not kind. Please don't leave your friends behind if they are on a bad trip. Next topic, please do not abandon your dogs. We found at least 10 strays today. Ok then. One more thing, Sunshine has lost her friend John. John has brown dreadlocks. Please keep an eye out for John."

I began to smirk. Not becuz of the girl on the bad mushroom trip or the stray dogs named "ganja" but the fact that every other person here had brown dreadlocks and was probably named John. Really, how are you going to find somebody simply on the basis of brown dreadlocks? Ha ha. But the men in the circle aren't done talking. After the announcements, they invite us all the a universal ohm. "Close your eyes brothers and sisters, and join us."

128

"ooooooooooooooooooooooooooooooooohm."

"ooooooooooooooooooooooooooooooooohm"

Wow. 3000 people ohm-ing at once. Now that was pretty frickn' cool; to breathe in unison with many people at once. That doesn't happen that often. Hell yeah, I was feeling the unity, love, light, and all that. Who says that just becuz I am bitter 'bout most new age things, means that I don't feel the one and the love and the light? I feel it, when we're singing and meditating. I just don't feel it when we're bullshitting and pretending to be uber nice.

"ohhhhhhhhhhhhhhhhhhhhhhhhhhhhhhm"

Post-ohming, a tiny man dressed in green leotards like a baby peter pan, jogs around the circle with a tin in his hands to collect donations for the food. A sad sight it was when literally nobody plucked money into the tin and when hands were seen dropping an object into the tin, you could see that it was food stamps not dollar bills.

The way the food situation worked out was that every camp at the gathering had a kitchen. And every kitchen had to give food to the nightly communal dinner. And every dinner was served outta an ice cooler/chest. What else are you gonna serve with when yer feeding 3000 people? In each ice cooler was an assortment of brown rice a la curry, oatmeal slop, spaghetti slop, brown rice a la slop, and oatmeal slop. Slop after slop served into stained coffee mugs with political stickers, tupperware containers from thrift stores, camping bowls, and random cups stolen from Burger King or parental unit's houses. Little kids ate with hands. Vegans ate with chop sticks. 19 year old soul searchers ate with the spoons that were connected to their belt, chain wallet, and leatherman. I grabbed the oatmeal with my muddy hands and pigged out like my chubby body hadn't eaten for days. Chubby bodies can starve too.

Stuffed on communal kitchen brown rice love, Tracy and I did a synchronized yawn, and set out for a place to sleep for the night. Up yonder in the grassy meadows, we came upon the "turtle camp." Above an area of tents, was a sign with painted turtles on it. The turtle was attractive, thus inspiring Tracy and I to promptly lay our sleeping bags next to the camp fire/drum circle. In the center, a scruffy man sat on a log playing the guitar and singing Bob Marley songs. He sang Bob Marley songs the whole night as soul seekers tried to sleep and tripped out men with bugged eyes in white robes did non-kinetic drug dances dis-intuned to the soaring flames. I looked up at the massive stars and fell flat asleep to a scratchy pubescent-esque voice singing "get up... stand up... stand up for your right... get up... stand up... don't give up the fight."
Tracy and I did our pathetic cuddle routine, that was now, two days old. When I awoke in the

morning, she was long gone. I got up and went over to the kitchen area. Tracy comes running outta some unidentified tarp structure, wearing an apron, and gives me a humongous hug. "Uh" I say, all still in my I'm-just-trying-to-wake-up-mode. "Guess what Hermitt!"

"What? Uh...uh..uh."

"I joined the kitchen crew!"

Joining the kitchen crew for Tracy meant that she was about to devote her entire body, mind, and soul to this kitchen crew. To put all the passion she can put into making new flavors of oatmeal slop: meaning, I was kind of on my own. Sure, I could hang out at the kitchen all day, playing hacky sac and smoking pot. But I could do that in Amarillo, Texas or Trenton, New Jersey. I couldn't let my "soul seeker" lifestyle down. There were new age wingnuts to meet and crazy hippies out there ready to convince me of their new miracle cure for life. I hugged Tracy goodbye and told her I would be back at the turtle camp for dinner. It was time, today, to see what this Rainbow Gathering thing is about.

I trekked down back to the main road, in search of... whatever. Bored by the drum circle and pot smoking and scheezy hippie men trying to hit on little girls, and even more people in brown dreadlocks hugging each other, I kept walking. Eventually, I turned my head left and witnessed the greatest thing at the Rainbow

131

Gathering: the nic and at nite camp. The nic at nite camp basically consisted of one big ol' tent with about 50 or so crusty-as-all-hell crusty punks (you know, the kind who name themselves scabies, sport greasy falling over mohawks, and only wear old black carhart patch material). The crusty punks sat there all day long rolling cigarettes. Asking people for cigarettes. Giving people cigarettes. Large tin cans of top cigarettes and other handrolling cigarette brands were scattered everywhere. The crusty punks growled and yelled "fuckn hippie" underneath their breath. I wish I could have joined them, but they weren't really my thing either. I thought they were going to eat me alive. So I kept walking.

Up the road, there was a glimpse of heaven to be found: the barter circle. Ah, the roots of capitalism at it's finest. (capitalism originated from bartering, just to let you know, IE: Capitalism used to be a cool power to the people thang) the barter circle is where the real game was played. I was prepared, I had played this game before. I was born a hustler. Back in The Big City, I had purchased a few packs of amerikan spirit cigarettes knowing that I could trade some good shit for them. I knew there would a large amount of hippies who would try to quit smoking at the rainbow gathering, like all the other people on the planet who are trying to quit smoking too. amerikan spirit smokes, alongside the ever popular hand rolled cigarette, are the cigarette of choice for amerika's hippie population. What better place than to deliver alienated people in the wood's drug of choice. People had been at the rainbow gathering for literally months, and they needed their fix. Ha ha, I'm evil. But everybody is evil at the barter circle. I'm out to get mine and you're out to get yours. Oh yeah, we can all share and shit. But let's look at the things we are sharing, oatmeal slop, clothes we don't want anymore, oatmeal slop... but all these hustler people at the barter circle, weren't about to share. They were about to trade exquisite glass pipes for ounces of pacific northwest weed. Tie dye shirts for hemp beanies. Food stamps for necklaces. I took out the blue packs of amerikan spirits and all eyes were on me. I went up to a girl trading tee shirts and hats. I held the cigarettes in my hand which immediately prompted her to say "I'll trade." Her friend turned to her and said "hey I thought you quit smoking!" "yeah, but these are amerikan spirits" she gleed. Ha ha suckers.

With the tee-shirts, I went over to another group of people, and traded the tee-shirts for the knife. With the knife, I went over to some dreddy pseudo-hip hop boys and traded the knife for a skateboard deck. Fuck yeah. A couple packs of smokes for a nice skateboard. I dig this real-capitalism shit. I even had packs of smokes left that I traded for hats and chocolate. Yum. Energized by the hustler enigma, I left the barter circle and continued to roam on... back to the turtle camp where Tracy was all busy stirring some type of unidentified wheat product I sit and wait for the dinner to began, anxiously staring at all the smiling hippies, wondering if I am like them, even though I don't have a single word to say to them.

When it seems like dinner is about to be served, the entire kitchen team runs into the massive unidentifiable blue tarp structure. A few minutes later, they come out all smiley. They musta gotten stoned. Oh well. Tracy comes up to me, sits down, starts rubbing her hand on my thigh, and leans into my cheek and gives me a big ol' kiss. "I love you" she says. I smile, hesitantly, and hug her. *Was she on drugs? Did she just love me like a heterosexual rainbow sister? Or was she really a hot and horny lesbian who needed to get... it... on with I, the nervous urban hermitt in a baggy hooded sweatshirt?* Well, the answer is... the world will never know. After dinner, I passed out next to the campfire cuddling next to Tracy. In the morning, when I woke up, she was gone. She wasn't in the kitchen or in the blue tarp structure. I looked everywhere, and she was gone. It didn't seem like Tracy was coming back, so I strapped on my dirty blue jansport backpack and set out in search of something new. Since I didn't bring a tent, due to the fact that I didn't even own a tent, I set out first for a new sleeping location. Bumping into my scheezy 40 year old ish friend Brian, I asked if I could stay with him. Brian led me to his tent area. In the back, we set up a tarp that was to be my own personal sleeping headquarters. Brian said that he had the tent reserved for him and his lady "friend" with whom he was trying to get it on. Hmmm.

Once I had sleeping quarters, I went out on a big roaming adventure. There just had to be more than just people with brown dreadlocks out here in the woods. I walked up into the hills, where there were not that many people to be found. Along the way, I found punks who had built their own tree house. There was a pirate flag in the front. "ahoy!" they shouted. I smiled and kept on walking. Forward on, there were more and more punks hidden out in the bushes. Beyond that, there was nothing, except flowers, fields, and deer. I skipped and jumped and pissed and sang the confused wandering song of a 19 year old soul searcher. Dunno, I knew what soul searcher really meant, I just assumed it meant a spacey kid in a baggy hooded sweatshirt who was looking for the neverending meaning of life. Well, I didn't find it in the pretty field, so I kept on walking and wound up back at the main rainbow gathering. I walked past carnivore camp, Vietnam vets camp, the sprout camp, the rasta camp, the faerie camp. I met people named "water" "snow" and "sun." Danced underneath a rainbow colored tarp. Meditated. Slept. Jacked off. By the time I was done with my busy day, the "universal dinner bell rang" thus sending me off to the 3000 person + field to enjoy another curried rice meal and another ohm.

I left the universal ohm dinner early and went back to my little tarp space underneath the tent, to watch the sunset alone. This is when I began to horrendously cry and cry to the point that it sounded as if I was choking. *Ok Hermitt,*

135

you really have to admit it this time, not just to yourself when you have a silly crush on a girl, that you are a flaming homo and there is no way around it, ok? Capice my brain said to me. My brain was yelling. So I did the most cliché lesbionic thing that a kid could possible do, besides buy every Ani DiFranco album and become vegetarian: I cut off my dreadlocks. I said goodbye to 5 years of sporting the long hair that was oh so not I. I thought of Jane and how she probably did the same thing. I wasn't trying to be like her, I was trying to just relate. I yearned for Jane to be here so we could fuck all the straight people and make out in the woods. Obviously, that wasn't going to happen and I still had a spiritual agenda to fill out. My hair was now choppy and unbalanced. I decided to go for the full job and just shave the fucker off. Out of 50,000 hippies in the woods, the only people that had a razor, or at least that I could think of, were the hare krishnas. With this knowledge, I rolled on over down to the Hare Krishna camp to borrow a razor and shave the fuck outta my head.

"Can I help you?" the head Krsna dude said, as a throng of devotees danced, chanted, and rang bells behind him.

"Yes" I said "I was wondering if I could borrow your razor."

"And what for young lady?" he said, in a condescending tone. Anybody who calls me young lady obviously has no clue whatsoever about the throng of young boy dykes that are sprouting everywhere across this planet.

"Well, I am going through a spiritual cleanse. I just cut my dreadlocks off and I would like to shave my head as a new beginning!" I said, so innocently and young.

"I cannot do that."

"Why not?"

"Because you are a woman and a woman cannot shave her head. She looks ugly when she does so. You see those men dancing over there? Now they can shave their head, but since you are a woman you cannot do this. Why did you cut your hair off?"

Yes, this is exactly what the head hare krishna master said. I didn't say a word after that and just stormed off. How could a religion that serves yummy curry brown rice for free everywhere you go on this planet tell me that I am not allowed to shave my head simply because I was born with female genitalia? Of course I didn't know shit about the hare krsna religion at that moment at time except that I had been eating a lot of their brown curried rice since the days of being broke began. But after that horridly sexist experience, I wasn't exactly pro hare krsna and I wasn't exactly pro Rainbow Gathering anymore as well. Walking back to my lil' tarp space, all I saw were women with long hair and men who looked like white society's version of jesus with a bunch of wild golden retriever dogs along the way. Ugh, the 1997 Rainbow Gathering of Living Love and Light wasn't exactly the place to come out to yourself and the world as a big ol' queer. Boy was I a fool. The mind warp-ization of lesbianism = granola, birkenstocks, and hippie folk music was shocked as all shit. Lesbians don't go to the Rainbow Gathering. In fact I didn't really know where they went. I was on a high time mission to leave this land of hippies and get back to The Big City. I looked for a ride back everywhere I could. It was a très last minute decision, but very important for my spiritual grow, you know? Eventually I came upon Star's friend Forest, who was indeed leaving for The Big City the next morning. I hugged Forest with my heart's content and slept the sweetest sleep a kid like I could that starry night.

Forest had a run down, dented as all hell 1985 mini van. Along with the van came his chainsmoking friend Marco, and an uber anal dreddy hippie girl named Kate. Kate was all pro Rainbow Gathering and even has the essential hippie outfit down: patchwork dress, patchwork wool sweater, knitted rasta hat, birkenstocks, and attitude. She was straight outta a DANK PRODUCTIONS catalog. Meanwhile, all that Marco wanted to do was leave the woods. "First stop," he said "is Dairy Queen, then I'm gonna get me a pack of Marlboro cigarettes. I haven't had those in so long. Fuck those hippie cigarettes. And then I'm gonna get me a Snickers bar!" I shouted hurray while Kate bitched and moaned saying that she was only going to live off the sprouts she grew at the Rainbow Gathering Sprout Camp. Forrest was neutral and just along for the ride.

Once outta the woods, we came upon a small country town. And lo and behold, the 1985 mini van drove into the Dairy Queen parking lot. Wow, I hadn't been to Dairy Queen since I was 9 years old. When we all walked in, all the small town country folk were staring at us with total shock. This is when I actually felt the rainbow gathering love that everybody seemed to be talking about. Amazing, all I could see in the eyes of the 15 year old small town Dairy Queen employees was love. In fact, I saw love in every person I came across. How could I have these rainbow gathering love powers yet have such a loathing for the Rainbow Gathering and be purchasing a corporate fast food chain Butterfinger Blizzard? Life wouldn't tell me why, I just enjoyed eating Snickers bars with Marco, watching him chainsmoke, and smoking heaps of pot all the while trying to ignore Kate's you must only eat sprouts antics all the way back to The Big City. When I got home, I got a bottle of wine, a poetry journal, hid in my room, and listened to Jane's Addiction.

SOMETIMES LETTERS CAN BE AWARDS:

Dear Urban Hermitt,

This is Wanda here at the Bi-Coastal Association for Underground Lesbians writing to inform you that you have just won the "Baby Dyke of The Month" award. Congratulations! You have won this award due to your strong merit for cutting all your hair off, obsessing over a girl named Jane, and raving about how apricot beer tastes like pussy, even though you haven't actually tasted pussy yet, how cute! Baby Dykes are a prime target for the older dyke eye. Hopefully soon, you will be seduced with thick ravenous clits and bushes and pierced nipples to suck on, my little baby! Hurray!

Now that you are an Official Underground Lesbian, a new life is ahead of you. Be prepared to shack it up with hot babes you met at a local Lesbian Avengers meeting. Be prepared to pretend to be an activist so that you can get laid! You will live a life of shopping at local natural foods co-ops yet going out at night and drinking cheap vodka at your local cheezy dance club. It is the life of the hypocrite but you can always come back at people with this amazing phrase *i am an oppressed minority as well!* Or if you choose to live in the city, you can come back at people with *Girl, you don't even know!*

There are downsides as well when you are an Official Underground Lesbian. You will meet anal lesbians who except you to only live off tofu and raw carrots when you crave the occasional piece of pizza. You will date women who listen to really bad folk music. You will even date at least one woman who is going through her *Ani Difranco Phase.* You will meet lesbians who will have "save the environment" stickers on their cars. Yet, if you can live past these downsides you will meet an incredible amount of dykes with pussies that taste good. You will get exposed to real Riot Grrl Music. And most of all, you will live a life free from fucking and making love to those with mullets. However, we do warn you that some crusty punk Underground Lesbians do sport dreadmullets and rat tails. You do not have to stay away from them, we just caution you.

Congratulations!
Wanda Colebank
The Bi-Coastal Association For
Underground Lesbians
Oakland, Ca/Burlington, Vermont

15. AN INTERVIEW WITH AN ACTUAL, AUTHENTIC LESBIAN:

I just had to know more about this lesbian culture that seemed so new, bright, and shiny to me! But I couldn't just walk into a lesbian bar, put my arm around some foxy dyke, and say "hey baby, will you take me home and teach me how to fist, carpet munch, and aerobicize with dildos?" I had to take a more sly approach AKA: I lied. I wandered into the local feminist woman's bookstore and noticed that the person behind the counter was sporting a 1994 Ani DiFranco U.S. tour tee shirt, underneath her blue railroad stripped overalls. I suspected that this was a secret code outfit for the underground nation of lesbians. I came up closer, and noticed there was a button on her tee-shirt that said "I Love My Cunt." I blushed, and then proceeded to tell her the biggest lie ever: *Hi, my name is Hermitt, and I go to the University of Washington. I am currently taking a Gay and Lesbian Studies Class and we have to do interviews on that kind of culture as part of our final. And I was wondering if I could interview you, you know about the bookstore, and such?*

It was such an obvious lie since it was the middle of Summer, and that summer classes had just ended at The University of Washington. Plus, I had just gotten back from the frickn' Rainbow Gathering in the Woods, was wearing a ripped up purple Rasta hat, and looked stoned outta my mind. Nonetheless, the person behind the counter, agreed to the "interview." She introduced herself as Joy and invited me to interview her at the local vegan café the next day. (what was up with my entire life revolving around the vegan café that had such bland tasting food, that I was forced to bring in bulk bags of salt in with me every time I walked in the damn place?!!)

When we met up for the interview, she was still wearing her 1994 Ani DiFranco US tour tee-shirt with her mighty "I Love My Cunt" pin. She smiled and let the questions begin.

Hermitt: So, um. Could you tell me about Gay and Lesbian culture in the 1990's?

Joy: So you're assuming I'm a lesbian, are you?

Hermitt: Are you?

Joy: Yes I am, but not because of the tee-shirt I'm wearing. But anyways, I'll answer your questions. Gay and Lesbian culture is a complicated thing. Could you be more specific?

Hermitt: Uh, maybe you could tell me about lesbian culture in this city?

Joy: Well, that's a broad topic as well, you're going to have to get a lot more specific.
Hermitt: Uh..Uh.. could you maybe tell me about the lesbian culture that you're involved in?

Joy: First off, it's not lesbian culture I am involved in, but progressive dyke culture.

Hermitt: is there a difference?

Joy: Dyke culture is well, more progressive.

Hermitt: How, so?

Joy: it is, you just can't explain it. Lesbians drive Mercedes and Dykes drive trucks, maybe? I dunno.

Hermitt: so is it a class thing?

Joy: Nah, I'm a big ol' dyke, and I come from an expensive private liberal arts school in Connecticut.

Hermitt: Oh, I'm confused. Like, is it a dyke thing to go to a liberal arts school? Maybe you could tell me more about the progressive dyke culture you're involved in?

Joy: A lotta dykes go to Smith College in Northampton, I think. I just have a lot of dyke friends. I don't go to dyke meetings or social gatherings, and the "lesbian" bar in this town sucks.

Hermitt: Oh, well what do you and your dyke friends do with your time?

Joy: Everyday things I guess. I mean I work at a woman's feminist bookstore, so I'm around it all day. My friend Kay works at the Women's run sex toy shop, that's always a blast. And of course, I like sex. I guess sex is the only dykey thing I do. I listen to Ani DiFranco too, but that's so stereotypical and cliché. and that's about all. And oh yeah, the bookstore, but that's so cliché as well. I guess it's the dildos.

Hermitt: Oh, is the sex toy store full of this town's progressive dyke culture?

Joy: Yeah, you could say that. They've got all kinds of dildos. I got this double sided dildo the other day, where you can stick the dildo in two people. They've got handcuffs, vibrators, whips, lube, videos, tons of books. Not all people who go there are dykes though.

Hermitt: so uh, would you say that dildos and such are part of this progressive dyke culture?

Joy: Sure, I guess. Well not every dyke likes a dildo up her cootch I suppose. I like vibrators a lot more, I got this really compact travel sized vibrator called "pocket rocket" and I take it with me everywhere I go. I even used it in the bathroom on an airplane going to Chicago once. But this is all personal shit, I guess I should be talking about stuff for your class, like The Stonewall riots, Ellen coming out on TV, and Gay Pride.

Hermitt: Oh, no no, I can read about that stuff in books. I want to know about the stuff I can't read in books. Like when did you come out as a dyke?

Joy: Not really until I was in college. I was working for the college radio and ended up hanging out a lot with the girl who did the radio show before mine.

Hermitt: what was your radio show about?

Joy: It was a Glam Rock Show. 1970' s David Bowie kind of music. Well, the more and more we hung out, the more and more I began to get deep sexual feelings for her. One night we got a bottle of vodka, got really, drunk, and ended up making out. From then on, we became lovers. It was nice. I didn't really tell anybody I was gay, until we broke up. Then I was on the prowl, and decided to sleep with as many women as I could. I never shaved my head or wore rainbow pride rings. I just told people. Some were cool and some were not. My parents didn't freak out or anything, but I bet they wish I was with men instead.

146

Hermitt: did you sleep with lots of men before you came out?

Joy: oh yah. It was ok, I mean I had fun. But I was practically drunk or stoned every time I had sex with men, so that should have told me something. I don't regret it, in fact sometimes I still sleep with men for the fuck of it. I just prefer to be in relationships with women.
Hermitt: are you in a relationship with somebody right now?

Joy: Yeah, I'm dating this cool girl I met through some friends. She really tries too hard to be butch though.

Hermitt: what does trying too hard to be butch mean?

Joy: Oh, you know, she tries to take care of things, act like she's in control. She drives a pick up truck and works as a plumber, but she is secretly the most whiney and cry baby person I have ever gone out with. She writes me love poems about trees.

Hermitt: do you like butches?

Joy: I like everybody, but I really do love a woman who will put on a big ol strap on and fuck me good. But I do love all kinds of women. I'd probably call myself an andro dyke. But for the most part, I am Joy.

Hermitt: what is an andro dyke?

Joy: andro stands for androgynous. Like I am in the middle, not really butch or femme or anything of that. Sometimes i like to call myself a *robo dyke* because I like to wear nerd glasses and dance like a robot. Robo-Dyke pride! I have spoken!

HATE MAIL:

Dear Urban Hermitt,

We went out on a date a couple of months ago, where you took me to your room to make "stickers." Do you remember that? I bet you do. You even told me that the stickers we were going to make were going to be "political." We wrote go vegan on about 25 sheets of sticker paper, while we ate cookies with dairy in them! Anyways, I thought you were earnest and sincerely wanted to make political stickers with me. Well, I was wrong! As I was neatly writing suck my left one on an orange piece of sticker paper, you leaned in and tried to kiss me. I kissed you back, as you may know, because I was horny. But that was no excuse Hermit, no excuse of all! Why couldn't you have asked me out on a date instead of trying to be "political."

When we first met each other at the local Lesbian Avengers meeting, I really thought you were political. But as I went to more meetings, I started to notice that all you were interested in was flirting with all the dykes there, and doodling on our meeting notes! You never showed up at our protest rallies, but you showed up at our parties and drank all our apricot beer.

Who do you think you are? Just because you rebelling from The National Council For Rigid Gender Roles and are an Official Underground

149

Lesbian, doesn't mean you have to lie to us. I don't regret having sex with you, but I doubt if it was real sex since I thought I was having sex with a real activist. Go back to the bars Urban Hermitt. Go back to your fruity world and thinking that writing is somehow revolutionary!

It's Over,
You Know Who I am
The Big City USA

16. COMING OUT OF THE CLOSET POOR PEOPLE STYLE!

My heart was beating faster than the time I took ecstasy and held hands with Jane combined when I sat in the barbershop waiting to get my hair cut. This wasn't just any barbershop. It was the gay barbershop in The Big City's gay district. Rainbow Gay Pride Flags everywhere. Faggy Men on Cell Phones. Bars everywhere. And when it was my turn to get my hair cut, my "stylist" was the most flaming-in-that-stereotypical-RuPaul-kinda-way gay man that The Big City had. "well honey, what can we do for you today?" I took off my big purple hippie hat. "Oh my" my hair stylist commented "what do we have here...hmmmm"

I explained to him that I had cut my dreadlocks of at the Rainbow Gathering and that I wanted a flat top! Oh, my coming out to the world was so painfully obvious. But better with the gays than the straight hippies, I suppose. I bet my stylist had seen cases like mine many times before because he was very happy to shave my head into a stone cold flat top: the butchest hair cut possible! It was also très fun having my stylist go "oh my" the whole time he flashed his hands around and cut my hair with high spirited frenzy. Maybe I wasn't exactly coming out, but instead, I was saying goodbye to the hippie world and the holy books and the drugs. Maybe my inner bitter indie rocker would shine. Maybe.

Leaving the gay barber shop, I was still scared and immediately put on my big ol' purple hippie hat. With the hat on, I noticed walking down the street, lots of creepy hippie men seemed to come outta the woodwork, smile, and say "haaaay seeeeeeester." I decided to conduct an experiment. I decided to take off my hat. Hat free, and suddenly there were no more creepy hippie men, and suddenly a mass amount of cute dykes of all assortment were smiling at me. Could this be? No? the experiment continued. I put my purple hippie hat back on. With that, the creepy hippie men reappeared and repeated "haay seester" over and over again like this was a bad, bad nightmare. I breathed in and decided that the nightmare was over! I took the hat off for good and proudly walked back to my Food Services of America job, which was actually at an uber hip pizza place on the main gay freaky goth piercing/tattoo shops on every corner street known as Broadway. Yeah, I forgot to mention that earlier in the book. How obvious was it that I was gay if I was working at a gay pizza place for pete's sake?

All my disgruntled hipster co-workers looked very shocked as I walked into work. Everything was in slow motion. I could tell that they all knew. I walked to the backroom and Tony, the really flaming gay boy was busy chopping onions and tomatoes while listening to an old Erasure tape. "Well Well Well" he said "What do we have here! You cut all your hair off, now didn't you? Well, you know that girls are going to start hitting on you now!" I gulped and felt butterflies doing really neurotic dances in my beer belly. He knew. But I also thought that it was really silly that I had to cut my hair to "come out." Plenty of dykes have long hair and shouldn't have to cut their hair short to prove shit about their sexuality. However, it was rather important that I chopped my locks off, cuz I am butch as all hell. I was one of those people in long hair that looked really silly in long hair. *The butch lesbian in long hair syndrome.* It was quite tragic. It should have been put in a John Hughes movie in the 1980s so that people like me wouldn't have to go through this torture.

My manager was also flamingly gay, but more so in an annoying way. High Drama and High Maintenance were Claude's two favorite personality constructs. Claude not only possessed a loud squeaky scratchy voice but he also had a high bubble butt and chainsmoked Virginia Ultra Light Cigarettes like they were Cock. Pretty Short Cock. Hmmm. He sang loud RuPaul music, yes this is so stereotypical true, and talked a mile a minute. His reaction to my flat top was "Well

153

Honey, it's about time you got rid of those nasty ass pseudo dreadlock thingees! It's about time you got a clean cut. Now get to work!"

I grabbed a bus tub and went out to the dining room to clean up pizza plates and have people stare at me. It was pretty mundane until I went up to a certain table and came up to a certain person. That certain person was a very sexy babe who I had been keeping my eye on for a very long time. She worked at the massage place across the street, was of Hawaiian descent, and came to the gay pizza place at least once a week to meet lovers. Every week it was a new lover. The two lovers, both being gorgeous dykes, would fondle and rub while drinking their hefeweizen microbrew beers while I stared and secretly drooled at them. Every once in awhile the Hawaiian Masseuse Babe would look over and wink at me. Upon this winking I would get really shy, blush, and continue to deny my sexuality. But today, there was no turning back. I went up to her table to collect her dishes and she grabbed my hand. "Uh, hi" I said.

"I see that you have cute your hair" she said in a very seductive manner with a bunch of winks.

"Yes, it was time to cut the dreads off"

"Oh yes I see. You know" then she took a deep pause and looked directly into my eyes "when somebody cuts their hair, it usually means that they are going through very big changes."

"Yup, well I need to get back to work!" nervously I screeched.

"Ok, see you later."

The rest of the night was pure torture, tons of dykes would stare and stare at me with their heart's content. I didn't mind the lust, I just felt like I had come out to way too many people at once. I might as had rented out a stadium, invited the entire population of The Big City, and made a speech about how all I secretly wanted to do was taste a girl named Jane's pussy. However the pizza place didn't pay me enough money to rent out a stadium. So after work I mangled one of my co-workers to buy me a 40oz, and I skated on home.

When I got home I forgot that I lived with a bunch of straight white male hippie men, I was so got up in my I'm gay! I'm gay! I'm gay! Look at me, I'm gay! World that I totally forgot that the poor things existed. They piled up the entire living room smoking pot, and making weird grunt noises. When I walked passed them, instead of saying "Hi Hermitt, how was the Rainbow Gathering?" One of them said "So Hermitt you cut your hair, does that mean that you're a lesbian now? Heh heh! Does that mean you can bring us home extra chicks! Heh! Heh!"

"Fuck you!" I growled.

"Chill out sister" the heathen said. Ugh. I

155

couldn't believe this was actually happening. This was like an after school special on TV. This is what the mainstream drug counterculture wanted but this isn't what I wanted. I passed on the pot and the 40 oz in my hand, went into my room, and wondered what I'd have to do next in order to figure it all out sans "the hippies."

I wrote reactionary poems:

Driving in my mother's suburban volvo (listening to the Dr. Laura talkshow) my mother says "so, your sister's volleyball coach is gay."

"so."

"oh well, he was in the gay olympics and I just love the way he flaps his hands... and he tells me that in gay relationships, one person is the girl and one person is the boy. Which one is you?" my mother says this like now she's suddenly the expert on what it's like to not have heterosexual privilege. "So, which one are you? Cuz I think you're the boy."

And all I can say is that I DON'T KNOW. At 9, I passed as a boy, renaming myself Paul so that I could play in the woods with the boys....But, at 10, I fell in love with New Kids On The Block and wore neon pink. I secretly thought I was a fag. It was pop culture burnout and all I could say was I DON'T KNOW.

I used to think I'd just be a cross between a 13 year old skater boy and a rasta queen but then I found out that the rastas were really homophobic, and I just like girls. So denying the rasta in me, I thought: is there a support group for in the closet pothead dykes who fall in love with straight girls?

But in the back of mind, everybody screams ARE YOU THE BOY OR THE GIRL?

And I was thinking of saying: CALL ME KID! Call me something you could never put in the personals of the Dear Savage Love Column. Call me slacker for even cow girls get the blues until I run away to the woods to pretend to be a cowgirl until I find out that in this reality, cowgirls like guys and don't eat peyote buttons. This fantasy sucks ass!

So then I discovered gender bending and Kill Rock Star Bands. I thought "aha! I have it figured out! I'll just become a transgendered punk rocker. My three week Hello Kitty girlfriend at the time said she was a transgendered punk rocker too cuz she was secret a drag queen due to her vast consumption of eyeliner. "Kiss me like a butch" she said and I thought: am I really kissing the spirit of a drag queen?

Ah!

Call me kid mom! Call me kid gay olympic

volleyball coaches, rastas, and 13 year old skater boys. Call me sapien with a homo. Call me another sucker who will get drunk ass at gay pride again this year.

I stomp on HE and SHE. I take some quiet time, running away to the woods again. I listen to the sounds of the frogs fucking in the pond. I do not ask the frogs if they are THE BOY OR THE GIRL. I just know that they are FUCKING!

Hell yeah, I get weirded out when you call me HE/SHE/or LADY or MAM. It sounds too prestigious like I need to learn which fork is the salad fork at some Sunday brunch. Hell yeah, I get weirded out when sexist men hit on me after 5 minutes of meetin me. I forget that this guy sees me as a lady cuz either porno or bible school told him so. I forgot that KID is not a gender in the Webster's Dictionary. But still, there's a voice in the back of my head that says just call yourself a cabbage patch kid.

AN ANGRY CO-OP SHOPPER WROTE ME A LETTER:

Dear Urban Hermitt,

I don't understand why you write all this trash about hippies when I saw you just last week at the natural foods co-op buying bulk organic hemp flakes. God, I wouldn't be writing you this letter if you were just buying something like bananas or bread at the co-op, but organic hemp flakes? Come on! What in the hell are you going to make with organic hemp flakes? Are you going to make hemp brownies? Are you trying to impress some "earthy" hippie lesbian with your hemp foods? Maybe you should stop and check yourself before you make fun of the people who do the same thing as you: buy fucking hemp flakes!

—Anonymous/Seattle

159

17. CREEPY HIPPIES FUCKING YOU OVER IN THE ASS DOES NOT FEEL GOOD:

I was minding my own business, jacking off and listening to the new Dj Shadow album in my room when Randy runs in with shortness of breath and a red face. He told me that I got get lot's of money if I talked to this "dude" who was from South Africa, standing outside our communal urban hippie house. There was a look in Randy's eyes that had this promise that maybe, just maybe my broke ass wouldn't have to slave anymore days at the Food Services of America Job. Or maybe it was that I was really really stoned (cuz masturbation and good hip hop always tastes a little more better when stoned) I went outside to discuss with Mr. South Africa. He told me that if I showed him that I had money in my bank account, he would give me money that I could donate to a charitable cause since he had to leave for South Africa tomorrow. "Why my bank account?" I asked. "So I can trust you" He said. I didn't know about this. Randy told me to trust him with "kind hippie" eyes. Mr. South Africa also had a sidekick lady next to him who kept nodding and saying "he does wuuuuundors!" I felt like I was in a Billy Dee Williams Malt Liquor commercial and boy, I was stoned outta my mind.

But being the dumb ass that I am, I trusted Randy with my money and showed Mr. South Africa my money outside of a bank ATM a few blocks away from the hippie house. I took it out of my account but I didn't hand it over to him. It was at that point that I waked up from my bad marijuana comma and realized that I was being scammed. With this realization, I put my money back into my pocket and proceeded to leave the situation. But then Mr. South Africa pushed me, and grabbed his greedy little hands into my pocket and stole all my cash from me. "fuck you!" I growled. "No dude" Randy said "You need to trust this man, he is wise dude." "fuck you!" I screamed again, to which the lady sidekick replied "he's wuuundorful!" like she was on crack. They were all on crack, but when It comes to my money, I'm on crack.

For a third time I screamed the helpless words of "fuck you." I didn't get the responded I wanted. Mr. South Africa stuffed a big wad on something inside a handkerchief under my arm, claiming it was money but by now I knew it wasn't money. "Now I want you to get the fuck home and don't you dare move the handkerchief

161

under your arm or I'll shoot you I have people watching." Mr. South Africa said, but this time in a non-south african accent. Randy smiled at him and said "trust me." I growled.

Shit.

Surprise, Surprise, when I get home and open up the handkerchief wad, strips of phonebook paper fell out. I flipped out and cried, screaming a many nasty things about all these hippies who had took over my precious innocent 18 year old life. When Randy came home, I went up and started hitting him and yelling "you fucking scammed me!" Of course Randy completely denied everything. By now I was on to him and his crystal methamphetamine game. I went back into my room and moped all alone like the good little urban hermitt that I am. I kept running the situation over and over again through my mind about how I got all my fucking money scammed, but all I really wanted to do was make out with Jane, the girl who turned me onto Ani DiFranco even though that she didn't know that she had turned me onto Ani DiFranco.

Broke, angry, and let down by the whole nightmare hippie thing, I had to move out right away. I rang up my pseudo-girlfriend Natasha and asked if I could crash on her couch. She enthusiastically said yes. Thank gawd she was a preppy fag hag. When I arrived at her doorstep with my trusty milkcrates full of tattered clothes and books, I realized that perhaps I was even getting myself into a more complicated situation than I thought. Natasha was living with her boyfriend Colin, my friend Docia's boyfriend Steve, David (the guy Nastasha attempted to hook me up with), a crackhead in the basement, and Timothy the uber faggy boy who had eyes for me the second I knocked on the front door. I swore Timothy was gay, but one night he came home with some beers which led to making out on the couch I was crashing on which led to sleeping in Timothy's room. Needless to say, I was no longer crashing on the couch. I was getting it on with Timothy and sleeping in his room.

Now I know what your are thinking, dear reader, Hermitt, didn't you just give yourself a flat top and come out as a dyke? True. I wasn't sucking Timothy's cock or anything. We just made out and cuddled. I thought he was a total fag the whole time. Everyday after work at the gay pizza place I would tell him about all the cute dykes I saw that I wanted to fuck. He listened and told me to just go fuck a dyke, but I was homeless and he was a place to stay. Being a slut does not file under "cuddling" and "kissing." Being a slut is sucking Timothy's cock and I did not do that. In fact, I was probably using him a bit since Natasha was caught up in sucking her boyfriends cock like Docia and I really needed to stay away from the crackhead who lived in the basement. David was never home. All my other friends were hippies that I was trying to avoid them, thus it was me and the faggy boy.

At work I was starting to have a stalker, a chubby girl in a baseball cap who would come in everyday and order two slices of cheeze pizza. She would always give me the eyes, but at the gay pizza place everybody was always giving each other the eye. It was only one day that I was out moping the dining room floor and singing The Cure out loud, that the stalker came up to me and gave me a piece of paper. I opened it up and it said "Karen 861-6790." Nobody was ever that forward with me. Was that what being gay was all about like all the silly Hollywood movies had told me? I look up to the stalker girl and rolled my eyes in a confusing way. I didn't know what to do. She rolled her eyes back and walked out the doors of the gay pizza place. At that point, in my head, The Pet Shop Boys music was blasting, gay pride flags were flying everywhere, and the world was spinning! After I got off work, I marched on down to the music store and bought my first Ani DiFranco CD ever "Like I Said" alongside with a blank tape. Then I marched onto the bus stop and got on. To my surprise, I bumped into Claude, my big butted anal gay boss at the homo pizza place. "What you up to?" I asked. "Oh you know, going up to Changes (Changes was a big ol gay bar near where I was staying-ed) to hang out with the boys." For the rest of the bus ride, Claude chatted away about how his true love was not pizza management, but acting. Pizza was only to pay the bills, but the stage was the love of his life. I nodded a lot and agreed with him but the whole time I was thinking oh I can't wait to get back to where I am staying and listen to the Ani DiFranco album, I wonder what it sounds like.

Back at Timothy's I anxiously put the Ani DiFranco Cd on and danced away to my lil' hearts content. Nobody was home, so I could get away with such behavior. It was quite silly, I was wearing my culturally appropriated Guatemalan pants and smelling my armpits the whole time. After an hour of intense woo-woo lesbionic dancing, I took out the blank tape I bought and set out to make a mix tape for Jane. Coincedentally, I was wearing my Jane's Addiction tee-shirt at the time. Of course, at that time, I wore that shirt every single day. In fact I wore the same Jane's Addiction shirt everyday from 15 to 20, when I had a funeral for it at the dumpster in the alleyway. The mix tape was going to be a way to tell Jane how I really felt for her. Even though she was miles away I thought that maybe the tape would wince her back to The Big City where she would commit to me and we could live in a hardwood floor apartment in the gay district. I had a plan, the tape was going to be a mix of techno, and lesbionic folk songs.

Aphex Twin
Ani DiFranco
Dj Shadow
Tracy Chapman
The Future Sound of London
Kd Lang

The Chemical Brothers
Joules Graves
Dj Wally
And so on....

I drew trippy little designs on the tape package, wrote her a note about loving life, packaged it up, and dropped it off at the mailbox. I was proud of myself, especially for putting the Tracy Chapman song on the mix tape that went no words to say the feelings inside I have for you, deep in my heart.. .deep in my heart. I also put on the Ani DiFranco song that went I wonder what you look like under your tee-shirt. I wonder what we have when we're not wearing words. I was feeling hella gay until Timothy walked through the door and reminded me of the trouble that I had gotten myself into. We went up to his room to listen to Stereolab, talk about philosophical books, and make out. It was the usual nightly routine. Coincedentally, Timothy asked "Hermitt, why in the hell do you wear that worn out Jane's Addiction tee shirt everyday?"

"Cuz I like it?" I simply responded which wasn't good enough cuz then Timothy said "Why don't you dress more retro? My ex girlfriend was a lot like you except that she dressed retro. You can get your retro clothes at Urban Outfitters." I didn't respond, I just pushed his little body down and kissed him. We had a habit of kissing for 4 hours straight. This time we kissed until the sun rose. Timothy pushed me down and started eating me out. *Lick lick lick.* That felt good. He used a neat trick that I still use till this day: when you start playing/eating out a cunt and it is dry, take your spit and smear it around to create a juicy effect. Then he looked up at me and asked me if I wanted to have sex. We had not had sex yet, so this was a big deal. In fact, I was a virgin which was even a bigger deal. Of course I am not one of those people who wait for the right one like I was going to get fucking married or something. Therefore, I looked up at Timothy's faggy face and said "why the fuck not, just remember that I am a virgin." With that, a serious look invaded his face, he whipped out his cock, and stuck a red rubber on. He stuck that thing in my little hole and began to thrwat back and forth like we were on a teeter totter. He wasn't talking and I was laughing maliciously the whole time. Losing my virginity hurt as expect, but more so it hurt in that way that I realized I did not like having sex with these penis things. In my head I was saying to myself *I'm free! I'm free! I admit to myself I am a dyke!* Ok, so I had already admitted that a few weeks ago at the 1997 National Rainbow Gathering of Living Light and Love. This time, I was just super-dooper validating it. But my freedom soon dwindled as Timothy said "this isn't working I can't get in you. Maybe you should start masturbating with a zucchini at home." Then he got up and left for work.

I don't have a home and I don't masturbate to vegetables, fucker. I got up and left for work.

167

The gay pizza place was all that I had left in the world besides my Ani DiFranco CD. I wanted to die, in that way that I really didn't want to actually die, I just wanted all the stupid shit to get out of my life. It was all negative emotions for me until I looked up at a girl with big shinning blue eyes. She introduced herself as Amber. She smiled and invited me back to her place to "hang out" after I got off from work. Girls were being so forward with me. It was crazy. People always say it's the gay boys who fuck each other all the time and really forward and that the lesbians don't fuck until 5 months later. The people were wrong! They all must have been on drugs or something.

I knocked on Amber's front door, anxiously awaiting what was going to happen. Kindly, she greeted me into her new agey studio apartment and brought out a little metal pipe. She filled it up with green bud and shoved it in my face. I was so scared to smoke pot again, since the last time I was stoned I lost all my money. Still, I smoked the pot anyways, in order to impress this beautiful girl with big blue eyes. Stoned, we ate cookies and stared into each others eyes. "Can I do some spiritual work on you?" Amber said. I agreed.

"First off" she said "close your eyes" I closed my eyes then Amber started touching and caressing my hands. "I'm trying to feel out your auras" she said. I dunno bout that, but it sure felt good. The feeling good continued as we exchanged sweet, short kisses. After a round or so of the sweet short kisses, Amber freaked out on me and told me that maybe I should be leaving right now because she had friends coming over. That didn't bug me too much, I had a pseudo-boyfriend to come home to. My brief encounter with Amber was bizarre, but also was a part of the package deal I got after I dreamed of gay pride flags and purchased my first Ani DiFranco CD.

Back at Timothy's in the evening, I was immediately informed that Timothy was not talking to me and he thought I was "trite" and "ditzy" and "uninteresting." Pissed, I went back to sleeping on the living room couch instead of Timothy's crusty green futon. I asked Natasha what had all happened. "Well," she said "Timothy didn't know you were an actual virgin, you lied to him! In fact, you lied to everybody!" "I did not!" I snapped back. "well, I thought you lied too" she added, and then stormed off back to Colin's room for a night of buttrock music, fucking, and weed. The next day, I took my latest paycheck from the gay pizza place and moved out.

THE LIBERAL ARTS COLLEGES IN THE WOODS ARE SENDING ME JUNK MAIL:

Dear Urban Hermitt,

Have you ever considered receiving your education from A Liberal Arts College in The Woods? Are you tired of overcrowded community colleges? And big league Universities who *don't understand who you are?* Have you ever wondered what "Post-Anarcho-Marxism" means? Have you ever wanted to learn about "Social-Primitivism-Ecology?" Would you like to get a degree in such things as *Astrological Puppet Therapy* and *Karl Marx as An Art Form?* Here, at The Liberal Arts College in The Woods, you can either live off student loans or your parents, while spending your days reading books on theories while smoking pot, drinking coffee, and hanging out with mostly white people! We exist all over the country, and are looking for privileged hippie white people like you. You don't have to feel lost or isolated in the world when you have Liberal Arts Colleges in The Woods by your side. And when you graduate, or even drop-out from one of our many forested locations, you can thank us for the use of words such as "counterculture," "theory," and "neo-primitivism." After your time with us, maybe you will work at a bookstore or make coffee. Maybe you will become a Communist or move to a Commune. Whatever your path in life may be, remember that we are the ones who put the "D" in Diversity. Enclosed is our catalog featuring our new course *Understanding Ecology Thru The Writings of Emma Goldman*. We hope you will consider us for your educational needs.

Personal Regards,
Yolanda O'Brien
Executive Director
The National Program For
Liberal Arts Colleges in The Woods.

18. AN INTERVIEW WITH AN ACTUAL, AUTHENTIC REAL LIFE EX-HIPPIE:

And on the 34th day of the 19th year of a kid named Hermitt's existence, a prophet came out of the front doors of the local natural food's co-op, and sat down next to Hermitt on a mid summer's day. Hermitt was just hanging out and enjoying a nice organic peach, when the prophet introduced himself as Ray. "Well, hello Ray" Hermitt said. Ray said hello back and began to tell truths of a thang called modern day hippie culture. The Hermitt wondered if Ray was psychic and could magically tell that The Hermitt had just been let down by an onslaught of hippies. Who knew. Hermitt just took it all in, and asked Ray for an interview, on the basis that he was an official and authentic ex-hippie himself. Hermitt felt like an ex-hippie as well.

Hermitt: So Ray, why do you feel the need to tell me the truths of being an ex-hippie? What is going on here?

Ray: Well, I used to see you come in the co-op a

few months ago when you had those pseudo dreadlocks, wore that hideous purple Rasta hat, and bought the hemp-rasta-seed energy bars. Those energy bars are a crock o' shit, I think DANK PRODUCTIONS makes them. Anyways, now I see that you have a flat top, don't buy the hemp-rasta-seed energy bars, and always give Madeleine, the lesbian behind the deli counter, the sexy eye. From that knowledge, I could tell that you were probably shedding from some of your hippie ways.

Hermitt: I see, but why is it important to tell me this knowledge?

Ray: Because I used to be where you were at kid. I believed in this false hippie utopia, but that doesn't exist. However, I think it's important to not get bitter when you are transforming from an idiot hippie kid to a fully functioning ex-hippie. I don't want you to start chainsmoking, only listen to goth music, and hating everybody. It happened to me and it can happen to you.

Hermitt: Why thank you for taking the time out of your busy day at the local natural foods co-op to Save Me. Do you think that I am showing any signs of this chainsmoking-goth-hate people behavior, and if so, what can I do to cure this?

Ray: No, I don't see this behavior in you, that's why I am trying to get you before the other subcultures try to get you.

Hermitt: Whadda ya mean about the other subcultures trying to get me?

Ray: Oh, you see I have been there and done that. I am 35 you know.

Hermitt: no way

Ray: Yes way. But, after I quit the hippie lifestyle, I did a complete polar opposite and became a rockabilly greaser. I gave up my organic raw foods diet, and started to eat hamburgers and drink half racks of Pabst Blue Ribbon beer. I stopped riding my bike around, and instead drove a 1967 Chevy Impala. I stopped listening to my trance music, and only listened to Social Distortion, and Rocket from the Crypt.

Hermitt: How long did you go through that stage?

Ray: A couple of years, until I started dating this boy who was a self described "eco-punk-anarchist." He listened to loud hardcore screaming music, wore these dirty brown carharts, ate out of the Trader Joe's dumpster, and wrote zines on things like making your own compost, and how to silkscreen.

Hermitt: That stuff sounds really cool.

Ray: Yes, it was cool. I quit eating hamburgers, made zines myself, and ran around with his pack. I really did love him through those years. But the problem was that even though him and his friends were doing great things, they were all the same. They were all white and male. They only wore carharts and only listened to hardcore. There was no variety, and in the end I was looking for more.

Hermitt: so then what happened?

Ray: I returned to some of my hippie ways, cuz I was looking for something deeper in my life. Then I bought a plane ticket to Thailand, and traveled around Asia for 6 months. I hiked, ate street vendor food, meditated on the beach, and met tons of people. It was one of the best learning experiences. When I came back to the U.S., I decided to just become a person. I wasn't a hippie, a rockabilly, or an eco-punk anarchist. I like to eat hamburgers, but I ride my bike everywhere and support local co-ops. I like to dumpster dive but I own yuppie furniture from IKEA.

Hermitt: So then, what is your point?

Ray: Well, that everybody goes through their phases, but if you are constantly the same stereotype/subculture your whole life, and everything you do has to fit that, then you're an idiot who needs to grow up. All I am saying Hermitt is don't let the Punks take you, or The Ravers, or Yuppies, or anybody. Do not let anybody take you in. I have spoken.

I WROTE A LETTER TO SOME DRAINBOWS:

To the stupid Hippies, (not all hippies are stupid)

I've finally figured it out! The movie "Dazed and Confused" and 30 dollar Grateful Dead tee-shirts are all just a marketing ploy by the "biggies" in Hollywood to suck all my hard earned money and make me a fool. Don't worry hippies, I won't be purchasing a 200 dollar Charlie's Angels bong at the local corporate headshop anytime soon. However, I don't understand how your counterculture can produce so many creepy sexist men. And I really don't understand how your "compassionate and accepting" lifestyle is mostly full of heterosexual people. There is nothing wrong with heterosexual people at all, in fact some of them are really great buddies of mine.....But, hippies there's only about 3 faerie fag camps in the U.S., one we'moon lesbian separatist community in Oregon, and that's all! But hippies, I don't believe in lesbian separatism communes, and I don't want to be the only dyke on a holy fagatarian land, ok! I am not your "sister." I am not your "mamma." I am a tomboy who like patchouli, pussy, and natural foods co-ops. Diggit? Word!

The urban hermitt!!

19. FAKE DICK TASTES LIKE...

I sat alone in the kitchen eating peanut butter and jelly in my new house obsessively listening to Ani DiFranco and waiting for Jane to write me back, dreaming that she had made me a mix tape too! I was completely absorbed in my own world until a short, hairy man comes walking into the kitchen. I hadn't met any of my roommates yet, since I just moved into to the boarding house in the ghetto yesterday, on a whim. The short hairy gay man comes up to me and smiles. "I'm George" Immediately after that, George opens up a kitchen cupboard and takes some food out. I look over only to see about 60 cans of USRDA food bank canned salmon! Bizarre. George opens up a can, mixes it in a bowl with food bank fish from the fridge, and starts to chow down. I am staring at this bizarre eating mannerism, but George thinks that I am staring at the taboos on his legs.

"Do you like this tattoo?" George asks. The tattoo he was talking about was a big ol' Japanese symbol. I didn't know what it meant.

"Sure, but what does it mean?" humbly, I ask while now staring at the food bank salmon clenched in between George's teeth.

"It means goddess."

"Oh I see." Why did a fuzzy little gay man have a tattoo that said goddess? I start to observe other tattoo on George's body in an attempt to figure him out. On his right shoulder, is a big huge women's symbol with a fist inside.

"What's that tattoo for?" I ask. George informs me that it was a tattoo that his last witch girlfriend made him get. "I just love women who are witches" he professes. Now I was really confused, because George really did seem like a gay man to me but here he was sporting goddess-feminist tattoo and talking about how he likes to date woman witches? Yes, I was being stereotypical and judgmental. But you see, I was in a world of gay pride flags, not open-minded gender-bending sexuality. Dig? Well, after my questions, George excused himself back to his room, and left me back to my peanut butter and jelly and Ani DiFranco music.

"So you like Ani DiFranco. Eh?" a red head girl said, as she opened the front door. She introduced herself as Nicole, one of the other roommates I had yet to meet. Nicole immediately informed me that she only listened to Brit Pop and Team Dresch. "I also own every single

Morrissey and The Smiths album ever made." She bragged. I followed Nicole into her room only to witness poster after poster of Morrissey. She was obsessed and it this was easily a good thing, it is much better to be obsessed over Morrissey than it is at being obsessed with trying to get in every girl's pants aka: the creepy hippie men. It was so bizarre to immediately be removed from the hippie world and to be put back in with other people.

"So what do you think of living here, did you just move in?"

"Yeah, it's kinda weird. I just met George. I watched him down canned foodbank salmon. But there's something really strange about him."

"Do you know?" Nicole asked, with a horror movie-esque look on her face.

"Know what. That he eats weird?"

"You don't know, do you?"

"On with it!" I demanded. Nicole licked her lips, rolled her eyes, and told me that George used to be a woman. He was a female to male transsexual. "And not only that, but George was this big ol' butch lesbian who got a muscle disease and had to take hormones to cure it. Since he was taking hormones, he decided to become a man!" Nicole added. Well, that explained the goddess-feminist tattoo and the witch girlfriends. I was shocked and speechless. Coming out as a big ol' queer was a big deal already, and this was something that blew my mind. Something I only saw on Donahue and Oprah tv talk shows. This news didn't make me scared of George in the slightest, it just made me more curious.

The next time George went out of his room to go to the kitchen, I came up to him with a chirpy yet oh so suspicious smile and said "So George, tell me about yourself!" I had to get to the bottom of this. Apprehensive, George told me that he was eating right now. So I watched him down food bank steak (yeah, so far, the only thing I really know about this guy is that he loves to eat foodbank meat products) and waited to ask questions.

"What do you do in your room all day?" I asked. Yeah, I was blunt.

"I am working on getting my PHD."

"In what?"

"Well Hermitt," George said nervously "are you queer?"

"Yes!" I said with pride. That was the first time I ever said that with pride too, and maybe that's because I secretly knew George was queer too.

"I am getting my PHD in transgender studies."
"Oh, interesting, why is that?"

At that, George informed me that he used to be Debra. Debra had a husband and kids. Then Debra's husband beat her, so she left him, and came out as a lesbian. Once a lesbian, Debra went to college all over the south, in hopes of someday attaining a PHD. While in Graduate School, Debra acquired a disease known as Lupus. In short, Lupus eats away all your muscle tissue, and taking hormone treatment is a way to cure it. Debra was feeling more than butch, and was looking to transcend gender a bit, which led Debra into becoming George. I asked George if gender was a lifelong struggle, and he told me that he was transgendered as more of a scientific experiment. He kept using the words WHY NOT? How come George was transcending gender in the name of science, and I was born a tomboy?

"You wanna learn a bit about transgender studies kid?" he asked. I nodded my head like a good young queer and followed him into his room. The first thing I noticed, was a bunk bed. Teddy bear stuffed animals dressed in S/M gear hung down from the top of the bunk bed. Some teddy bears even had dildos hanging down from them. It was surely the strangest thing I have ever seen. Sex toys and books on every topic associated with transgenderism you could think of piled everywhere. George rolled up his pant legs, showed me his thigh, and explained that every week he would inject hormones (otherwise known as testostorone) into his upper thigh. He showed me the needles and the little vials full of the hormone drugs. The whole experience was more scientific than emotional: inject the drug into your body and get more body hair. I had so many questions to ask, but he never answered them. George would only show things.

In the next few weeks, George and I quickly became friends. We drove around in his little mustard yellow Datsun car, and explored the world. We had a lot in common, the main thing: being poor. Funny how being poor transcended our gender, sexuality, race, hobbies, etc. George showed me the world of foodbanks in The Big City, even though I passed on the food bank meat. He took me to all the queer thrift stores, pointed out all the stores that were really just fronts for S/M clubs. He pointed to me people and asked me if I knew they were female or male. I couldn't answer the question. From then on, every person I saw, I couldn't assume anything about them. Were they gay or straight, born a woman, man, or intersex? I was sure as hell confused.

One day, I told George that my head hurt from all the confusion. I had been lied to about gender. He told me it was going to be alright, then trudged on down to the local ghetto mini mart, and got me a 40oz of Olde English Malt

Liquor. I sat in his room, listened to Tracy Chapman, and stared at the moon. My confusion was starting to go away, not because of Tracy Chapman folk music, but because staring at the moon is something that grounds me, helps me focus. Plus, how can you not stare at that powerful shinning thing? I was in love with life, and George was smiling like maybe he was in love with life too? But when he whipped out a zip-lock bag full of psychedelic mushrooms, I knew that his smiles were all about the drugs. He handed me over a handful, and I got scared to put it in my mouth. I had already done enough drugs, my whole year thus far was turning out to be pretty-drug centric. But the mushrooms were a gift from my new queer friend, so I took them, grinding my teeth the whole time. When the mushrooms started to hit my head, George received a phone call from his long distance girlfriend and kicked me outta my room. I was alone and on drugs.

I went to the bathroom to take a big dump. Going to the bathroom, soon, became the hardest thing in my life. When I sat on the toilet, I started haullcinating and seeing skeletons everywhere. I tired to do what all the Holy Books that I had been reading told me to do, I tried to love the skeletons and becoming at one with the skeletons. The skeletons, however, were nor responding to my pleas, and kept on being creepy. I ran back to George's door and told him that I was having a bad drug trip. "I can't now Hermitt,

I'm talking on the phone with my girlfriend." To try to get a sense of peace, I went outside on the front porch and banged on my hand drum. That attempt at peace didn't last too long, for some neighborhood kids screamed: shut the fuck up! Stop playing your drum! We're trying to do our homework! People telling you to go away and shut up when you are paranoid and seeing creepy skeletons when you are on magic mushrooms tastes worst than the most unkept porty potty in the world. There was nowhere left to go but my tiny room. I hid under my blankets and put on The Beatles "The White Album." I figured that would be good drug music. John Lennon and Paul McCartney sounded ok, but when it got to Yoko Ono's guest appearance on the album, I was freaking out. Yoko Ono, at that time, sounded like the creepiest most scariest thing in the world. I turned the album off and grinded my teeth in bed the whole night, living in fear.

The next morning, when I awoke, finally sober, I decided that doing pyschedelic drugs was not the best thing for me. I wasn't getting enlightened and I wasn't feeling good. I wanted to finally figure it all out this time, and I meant it. Fuck the hippie and the drug bullshit! I hoped on a city bus and headed off to a meditation class I saw advertised at the local natural foods co-op. I was going to go the classic route, the Buddhist route, the route that had worked for so many people before me: sit down, cross your legs, close your eyes, and breathe!

The meditation class was in the basement of a library, in a cold damp room. When I got there, nobody was sitting on the floor and nobody was meditating. A bunch of random assorted people were seated in chairs while a tall man in a beard wearing a long white robe did a huge speech about love and consciousness. He could have been reciting Bob Marley songs lyrics for all I knew. Behind him, was a picture of an Indian (India as in the country) Man in a Turban. He was referred to as "the master." Every once and awhile the man in the beard would refer to the teaches of "the master." A tiny red haired lady stood next to the speaker and would say sporadically "look into his eyes! Look into the masters eyes!" Yo, this was no meditation class. Maybe it was a cult? Maybe I had walked into the wrong building and somebody was just filming a movie about cults?

When the bearded man was done talking, he invited people to come and meditate with him. Everybody in the room left but me. I didn't care if these people were crazy or not, I just wanted some guided meditation. But, the bearded man said that I had to do a meditation test where I would meditate for 3 hours straight, while everybody watched me. I didn't know if they were going to poison or shoot me, but I was so set on meditating on this godman-hungover from majik-mushrooms-and oppressive gender binary systems day, that I sat down in front of the lifesize picture of "the master," closed my eyes, crossed my legs, and breathed. The breathing was nice. That's all I can really say about the mediation. It was the longest I had ever meditated or sat still my entire life. 3 hours, isn't that what the real monks do out there in Tibet? Isn't that what Buddha did when he wasn't eating bowls of rice and telling all the impatient humans on planet earth to calm down? 3 hours was a lifetime, and I sure as hell wasn't enlightened, but I was calm. And that was good enough.

I opened my sore blue-light sensitive eyes, and the bearded man in the white robe was staring right at me. "So, how was it?"

"Nice"

"Can I ask you a few questions?"

"Sure"

"At any time at all when you were meditating, did you have any visions or see anything?"

"I dunno, I saw colors?"

"Did you perhaps, see a great Holy figure, like perhaps, the master?" he demanded.

"No master, I saw Jesus though." I lied a little bit. I didn't really have any great visions of Jesus, I mostly just tried to keep up with my breathe and thought a lot about the emotions of my life.

"You sure you didn't see the Master?" he demanded even more.

"No, I swear I didn't see the master." Man, could you give a kid a break?
"Well, that's surprising because everytime somebody meditates in front of the picture of the master, they have visions of him, but we will forgive you this time." He demanded harshly. Whoa I had just devoted 3 straight hours of my life to meditating in front of these crazy people that I didn't even know, and now they are mad at me for not having visions of this master dude? I was getting up to leave anytime now. I told the disciples of the master thank you and tried to head on out. They stopped me and said that there was a few more things to do. The lady in the red hair took me aside and whispered the master, oh he is wonderful. He does great things. you just look in his eyes and see so much love. And when you meet him, and he touches you on the head, you feel even more love. Oh the master! Master! Master! Now, I am not against holy guru healers at all, but something about being named MASTER kind of rubs me the wrong way. MASTER sounds like a slave master or dog owner or S/M buff who is going to give me a lotta bruises on my butt, not a healing person. The red haired lady wingnut was not convincing me at all. She

took me back to the group of disciples, we held hands, and they all shouted "oh master, oh master" like they were a cult because they were a cult and I sure as hell hoped that basements of public libraries were not the place where cults brainwashed you. After the "oh master oh master" chanting, the red haired lady took out of little plastic bag of puffed rice. "This rice is holy" she spoke as all the disciples in the room went ooooooh "This rice was touched by the master." She handed everybody a piece, they held the rice up in the air, chanted MASTER OH MASTER a million more times, and put the rice puff in their mouth. I didn't swallow my piece for I was scared it was laced with some drug so that the MASTER cult would brainwash me. I was through with drugs, even drugs that might be on rice puffs.

Before I finally got to leave, the disciples tried to convince me to stay on the MASTER'S commune out in the boomfuck sticks of Central Oregon. They said that if I stayed there, then I would learn to have visions of "the master" when I mediated. All that I had to do was wake up at 5AM every morning, live off only the food that "the master" told me to eat, and refrain from sex. It was also suggested that I pay 5 dollars a night to stay at the commune. I said thanks, but no thanks a million times, then ran out of the library as fast as I could. Phew.

Back at home, I only did one activity: eat

food. Doing anything else might have overstimulated my mind. It had been a rough few days. So I sat in my room, eat some curried coconut stirfry, and listened to the sound of the raindrops outside go drip drop drip drop. The phone rang in unison with the drip drop drip drop and I picked the phone up and said hello. The person said back hello hermit, it's jane. Oh Mi Gawd! I hadn't heard from Jane in months, in fact I never thought I would hear from her again. But here she was, calling me out of the blue.

"Uh..hi"

"Hi" I said back.

"I'm in town."

"Oh, what are you doing here?"

Jane said that she was only in town for a day, and that she was on her way a few hours down south to The Liberal Arts College in The Woods. Not just any Liberal Arts College in the Woods, but the same one that I went to. Jane said that she was just trying to figure it all out with meditation, experimental education, and vision questing. Whatever vision questing meant, all I cared was that she admitted that she was trying to figure it out like me, and that she had called. We didn't end up talking too much, it was awkward, and full of baggage. At the end of the conversation, Jane promised to see me again, and said "And by the way, I really really dug that mix tape you made me."

THE URBAN HERMITT STYLE DICTIONARY:

The Way:
A. The Drugs.
B. The New Age.
C. The Soul Seeker
D. The Kid who got dragged here.

4:20: smoke pot *dude* and make 30 dollar tee-shirts saying it.

Andro: No Gender. Can you even imagine?

American Spirit Cigarettes: the cigarette of choice for all those claiming to be "progressive."

Ani DiFranco: Folk musician who as inspired a generation. Known for her witty lyrics, and cheezy jazz voice that goes "Haaay uh aaaaay hay uh aaaay."

Aphex Twin: Most often referred to as the Philip Glass of techno musicians. He started making his own techno music and instruments at the age of 11. He reigns from Great Britain, lives in an old bank, and drives an old tanker as an automobile, because he can.

Black Market Bank: Making lot's of money under the table.

Boy Dyke: I am a dyke cuz my pussy rubs against another pussy when I make love yet I feel like a boy. Get it?

Butch: More masculine. Does not mean tough and drives trucks. Means more masculine. Wimpy poets who ride the bus can be masculine.

Butt-Rock Hippie: A person who truly believes they are a hippie but in the end, listens to a lot of Black Sabbath and Rush and does speed. Hippies who do speed. White Trash Hippies etc.

De La Soul: chubby rapper dudes from Long Island who rap about food, daisies, and chubby women.

Dear Savage Love Column: Gay man who writes love column. considered risqué by the conservatives.

Dildo: is not a fake dick. it is a phallus like creation that feel good.

Eco-Punk-Anarchist: A person who pretends to be vegan who dumpster dives, writes theories on how we are going to get free, and listens to loud thrashing music that is supposed to be about saving something though you usually can't hear the lyrics.

Edgar Allen Poe: Wingnut Poet on Drugs that kids in school are forced to read. Was considered a genius but while in school, his poetry sounds bad meaning: all drug poetry is awful.

Enya: New Age Music Artist. Sang in Volkswagon commercials.

Even Cowgirls Get the Blues: A Tom Robbins novel about a cool cowgirl with a large hitchhiking thumb who hooks up with rad lesbionic cow girls.

Faerie Fag: an earthy, spiritual gay man.

Fagatarian: Such a beautiful Fag!

Fag Hag: Woman who takes affinity and deep friendship and obsession to the fag she can never have. Kind of like a pseudo-girlfriend.

Femme: more feminine. Does not mean that is really straight. Does not mean only wears make up and dresses. Tough dykes who drive trucks can be femme.

Freestyling: Makin' the song up as you go!

GenderBending: Imagine a world free from baby boys wearing blue and baby girls wearing pink.

Grrr'd: You know how someone makes that "Grrr" noise? Well Grrr'd is the VERB of that.

John Hughes Movies: He was responsible for all the amazing pop movies in the 80's like "The Breakfast Club" and "Pretty in Pink."

Joy Division: Quite possibly one of the finest new wave goth bands of their time. The stuff intelligent depressed 15 year olds listen to. Surprisingly, the lead signer killed himself and his favorite music was reggae.

Kill Rock Stars: Cool Indie Rock label in Olympia that is responsible for Riot Grrrl and cool indie rock music everywhere.

Leeeeeezbuin: Somebody who is more of a lesbian separatist, refuses them to call themselves a dyke, and says that the word "dyke" is degrading.

Michael Bolton: Bad bad pop-romance signer of the late 80's who had long hair but was balding.

Munchies: Where you are very hungry and could munch on food items such a pretzels, chips, and pizza for hours.

Mullet: Short on the top. Long on the back.

Murder City Devils: Hipster Indie rock band from Seattle. Pabst Blue Ribbon Beer, Tight Pants, White Belts, and Tons of tattoo.

Neo-Primitivism: Can you please tell me what this means?

Phish: Modern Day Grateful Dead band from Vermont.

Pimp Status: When you have enough money to pay for everything to somebody who may not exactly dig you.

Po-Po: you're gonna have to listen to some gangsta rap music and then you'll know what this word means.

Post-Anarcho-Marxism: I really do not know what this means, probably a combination of theories on how to make the world perfect. The question is, do they really work?

Queen Latifah: bad ass rapper who don't take no shit. Many think she be GAY.

Riot Grrrl: Some smart people got together in Olympia in the early 90's. They made zines and cool bands like Bikini Kill.

RuPaul: Famous drag queen who sings cheezy house music. Had hit single "supermodel."

Sedona, Arizona: a place that some people think is spiritual and full of crystals out in Northern Arizona.

Social-Primitivism-Ecology: Yet another combination of theories on how to make the world perfect. Was the world ever perfect though, now that is the question.

Spirulina Green Algae that grows on the bottom of the ocean. High B12 and boosts your immune system.

Taurus: Astrological Sign of people born in Late April thru Mid-May. Stubborn and earthy.
The Cure: One of the greatest new wave goth bands of all time. Inspired the shaggy black hair-tight pants-big white sneakers look.

Tim Leary: That Harvard Professor that took way too much lsd in the 60's. Coined the phrase "turn on, tune in, drop out."

The Chemical Brothers: techno group that is famous.

The Gay Mall: A Mall that is gay people centric, usually including a cutesy store selling pride rings, and stupid tee shirts that say look! *I'm gay!*, a gym, a video store, a liquor store, The Gap, and so on. Gay Malls never exist in the suburbs.

The Smiths: The greatest Brit-Indie band of all time.

Trader Joes Dumpster: this is the dumpster that most who dumpster dive live off of. Thank you Trader Joe's!

Tres: is for "very" in French.

Trois: is for 3 in French.

Tupac: g-funk rapper from New York. Mother was a black panther and he was killed. can you make the colloration boys and girls?

Vegan: No Dairy. No Meat. No Whey. No Leather.

Wildcrafted Nettle Scrubies: Pick nettle in the wild. Nettle is scrubby so you can wash dished with it.

Wingnut: Damn you crazy.

Wraps: A yuppie way of saying "Burrito." However, wraps usually include spinach tortillas.

Yoko Ono: Stop singing!

Yoni: Pussy

The Way:
A. The People who think they are Punks
B. The People who think they are Hippies
C. The People who think they are Yuppies
D. The People who think they are just trying to make the best outta all this.

The urban hermitt hangs out a lot in the Pacific Northwest, a few hours south of Canada. Besides frantically writing the flow of life, the urban hermitt likes to shop at natural foods co-ops, take naps, listen to and perform hip hop, freestyle, skateboard, hug trees, and to be a zine geek. The urban hermitt also likes being in love. This is the Hermmitt's first book!

MICROCOSM PUBLISHING

A DIY mailorder! Hundreds of self released zines, books, records, movies, patches, buttons, stickers, t-shirts, bike tube jewelry, reusable menstrual pads, tapes, & more!

Send $1 for a catalog

We make custom 1" buttons, vinyl stickers, and canvas patches!

Stolen Sharpie Revolution a 96 page booklet documenting zine and DIY culture into one comprehensive manual. Also doubles as a how-to guide for various zine and DIY related projects including a pull out section with envelope templates. $3
"You NEED this" -Quimbys

The CIA Makes Science Fiction Unexciting #1 This zine explains the involvement of the CIA and FBI in the assassination of Martin Luther King Jr. It also covers destroyed evidence, bribed and threatened witnesses, and the process of implicating James Earl Ray as the patsy. $1 + 1 stamp

Urban Hermitt zines #8, 10, 11, 12, 13, 14 More of the Hermit's free stylin' chronicles in zine format. $2 ea.

Upcoming projects: **Brainscan #19** is about Alex's travels over the summer of 2002, the zine symposium, rock n roll camp for girls, and her introspective musings on it all.

Brainscan: Love Letters to Irony Book compiling issues #1-18.5 and more. Super fancy packaging.

How2 zine collection featuring #1 and #2 plus some new material as one volume. The covers will be screen printed. Over 168 pages!

503-286-1038   joe@microcosmpublishing.com
www.microcosmpublishing.com
Microcosm / PO Box 14332 / Portland, OR 97293